Corporate Governance

# Climate Change and Corporate Governance

**Please cite this publication as:**
OECD (2022), *Climate Change and Corporate Governance*, Corporate Governance, OECD Publishing, Paris, https://doi.org/10.1787/272d85c3-en.

ISBN 978-92-64-46186-4 (print)
ISBN 978-92-64-41729-8 (pdf)
ISBN 978-92-64-43320-5 (HTML)
ISBN 978-92-64-36159-1 (epub)

Corporate Governance
ISSN 2077-6527 (print)
ISSN 2077-6535 (online)

**Photo credits:** Cover © Fahroni /Getty Images.com.

Corrigenda to publications may be found on line at: www.oecd.org/about/publishing/corrigenda.htm.

# Preface

Rebuilding our economies following the COVID-19 crisis provides an important opportunity to transform production processes and consumption patterns in a way that mitigates the impact of climate change and related environmental degradation. Both our own well-being and that of future generations depend on it.

Businesses will play a critical role in this transformation, helping to achieve the goals that are set out in the Paris Agreement through innovation and investment. A successful climate transition will also require that companies address and manage any climate-related risks associated with their activities. It is critical that they regularly assess and disclose how they address climate change and the risks it poses to the sustainability and resilience of their businesses.

First, the framework for corporate disclosure of sustainability information needs to improve. Disclosure standards used by companies must ensure that the information provided is comparable and reliable. Second, company boards need to take account of the interests of all stakeholders, including on sustainability matters. The *G20/OECD Principles of Corporate Governance*, the leading international standard for corporate governance, highlight the importance of this, which is also the best way to create wealth for shareholders. Third, while many large companies already have climate transition plans, the mechanisms for shareholders and stakeholders to assess and engage with corporate boards to ensure that they are followed remain largely underdeveloped.

This report looks at the major implications of climate change for corporate governance and at some of the instruments that shareholders, boards and stakeholders can use in order to promote the corporate sector's role in limiting global warming. It also supports the work currently underway to revise the *G20/OECD Principles of Corporate Governance* with a view to help guide the efforts by policy makers and regulators to adapt corporate governance frameworks to better address climate-related challenges.

The revised Principles, which will be issued in 2023, will also provide guidance to support companies in the management of other risks related to their sustainability. The corporate governance framework advocated in the Principles also plays a key role in promoting corporate access to market-based financing, which will be essential to support the type of innovation and private investment needed in order to transition to a low-carbon economy. Consequently, the implementation of the Principles will not only improve the corporate sector's ability to contribute to the net zero transition, it will also make it more dynamic and resilient to future shocks.

I count on us collectively making the most of this important report and wish to thank the OECD Corporate Governance Committee for taking the leadership in the area of climate change and corporate governance.

Mathias Cormann,
OECD Secretary-General

# Foreword

*Climate Change and Corporate Governance* offers a comprehensive account of the main trends and issues related to the implications of climate change for corporate governance. It informs policy makers on some of the most relevant factors they should consider when evaluating and improving their legal, regulatory and institutional frameworks for corporate governance. This report focuses in particular on climate change challenges related to corporate disclosure, the responsibilities of company boards and shareholder rights.

The report also supports the OECD Corporate Governance Committee's ongoing review of the *G20/OECD Principles of Corporate Governance*, which is the leading international standard in the field of corporate governance. One of the most important issues under discussion is how to enhance the quality, reliability and comparability of corporate sustainability information. This is especially important for investors to better understand the risks they are facing and to efficiently allocate capital to the companies that are better able to thrive in a low-carbon economy.

The issues discussed in this report are considered within the framework of the broader discussion taking place on environmental, social and governance (ESG) risks and opportunities, focusing more specifically on climate-related ESG risks for two reasons. First, from a practical viewpoint, many governments, regulators and standard-setters such as the Financial Stability Board (FSB) have expressed a preference for initially focusing their attention and resources on risks deemed to be high priority by a great number of companies and investors. Second, it would be a much bigger and more ambitious task to attempt to comprehensively cover all aspects of ESG risks and opportunities in one sole report, particularly considering the complexity and variability of information available on different ESG topics (e.g. biodiversity and human rights). This focus on climate change provides an opportunity to look concretely at how current ESG frameworks for disclosure, consideration of risks and other corporate governance issues may be applied on a particular ESG topic.

This report was authored by Caio Figueiredo Cibella de Oliveira, Tugba Mulazimoglu and Daniel Blume under the supervision of Serdar Çelik. It benefits from discussions within the OECD Corporate Governance Committee and incorporates comments from delegates. The authors are also grateful for comments from the Responsible Business Conduct Centre and Financial Markets Division within the OECD Directorate for Financial and Enterprise Affairs, as well as from the OECD Environment and Development Co-operation Directorates. The report was prepared for publication by Pamela Duffin, Liv Gudmundson and Greta Gabbarini.

# Table of contents

## FIGURES



## TABLES

# Executive summary

Climate change is considered to be a financially material risk for listed companies that account for two-thirds of global market capitalisation. That is why climate change and associated risks are the number one priority for institutional investors when engaging with companies globally. However, corporate governance frameworks have not yet fully responded to the major challenges that climate change has engendered in relation to the corporate sector.

This report presents the main trends, issues and implications of climate change for corporate governance. In particular, it focusses on relevant developments for policy makers evaluating their legal and regulatory frameworks for corporate disclosure, the responsibilities of company boards and shareholder rights.

**Corporate disclosure**. While financial standards already require disclosure on how climate change may impact a company's business, a number of concerns have been identified with respect to the structure, comparability and reliability of such disclosure. For instance, as a rule, many financial standards do not require a structured disclosure on strategy, risk management and non-financial information (e.g. greenhouse gas emissions) that may be relevant for investors to assess a company's business and risks.

To date, a number of reporting standards have been developed for companies to disclose sustainability information but these standards vary with respect to their target audiences, the issues they cover and the threshold they recommend for information to be disclosed. This plenitude of existing standards also raises questions related to the comparability of sustainability information disclosed by companies. A lack of comparability harms investors' capacity to adequately evaluate companies when deciding how to allocate their capital and engage with these companies.

A growing number of jurisdictions have established regulations or initiated public consultations on proposals to mandate companies to disclose sustainability information according to a specific reporting standard. Many of these regulatory initiatives across OECD, G20 and FSB members have focused on climate-related disclosure requirements or guidance, frequently with reference to the FSB's Task Force on Climate-related Financial Disclosures (TCFD) recommendations to facilitate the comparison of sustainability disclosure between companies. Additional work is underway to align different standards under a single sustainability disclosure standard that would build upon the TCFD and other frameworks.

The use of multiple sustainability reporting standards is not the only barrier to greater consistency and comparability of corporate sustainability disclosure. When the sustainability information disclosed is not assured by a third party based on robust methodologies, this can undermine confidence in the information. Globally only around half of large listed companies that disclose sustainability information provide some level of assurance by a third party. And a majority of these assurance engagements provide only "limited" assurance reports.

Importantly with respect to any reporting standard, a key issue is the definition of which information is material and, therefore, should be disclosed. Information is "financially material" if it could reasonably be expected to influence an investor's analysis of a company's future cash flows. The concept of "double materiality", in turn, incorporates what is financially material, but also includes within its scope information relevant to the understanding of a company's impact on the environment and on society. This concept is new, and is not the standard in most jurisdictions.

While in theory clearly distinct, the frontiers between financial and double materiality may be rather fluid in practice. For instance, in what constitutes one aspect of "dynamic materiality", a risk that does not seem to be financially material at a moment in time may quickly become financially relevant, if for instance the social context changes. To some extent, therefore, the time horizon used in the analysis of materiality may also be key: the longer the time horizon, the larger the potential for overlap between financial and double materiality.

**The responsibility of the boards**. While business reality is complex, corporate law generally presents a simplified definition of directors' duties, including the duties of care and loyalty, in order to make them functional. These frameworks underlie an ongoing debate on how directors' decisions may reflect the interests of shareholders and stakeholders and how these interests may be balanced. Jurisdictions vary in relation to who is effectively the recipient of directors' duty of loyalty between the following two extremes:

- At one end of the spectrum, company law may fully adhere to the "shareholder primacy" view, obliging directors to consider only shareholders' financial interests while complying with the applicable law and ethical standards. This still requires attention to stakeholders' interests, but only to the extent that those interests may be relevant for the creation of long-term shareholder value.
- At the other end of the spectrum, directors need to balance shareholders' financial interests with the best interests of stakeholders, and, in addition, to fulfil a number of public interests.

Both models above have their advantages and drawbacks. Independent of these considerations, some companies are already actively integrating sustainability considerations into their strategies and executive compensation plans. Globally, 30% of listed companies with performance-linked executive remuneration use sustainability-linked performance measures in their plans.

**Shareholder rights and engagement**. With investors allocating a growing share of their portfolios to sustainability and ESG-related funds, shareholders have expressed a high priority in their engagement strategies to focus on climate-related concerns. In doing so, shareholders commonly use three main fora to compel companies to incorporate climate change considerations into their business decision-making processes: direct dialogue with directors and key executives, shareholder meetings and courts.

In shareholder meetings, shareholders may typically propose a resolution requiring a change in corporate policy, change the composition of the board or even alter a company's articles of association. By mid-February 2021, shareholders had filed 66 resolutions specifically related to climate change for the year's US proxy season (in addition to 13 proposals about climate-related lobbying). Twenty-five of those climate-related proposals asked for the adoption of greenhouse gas emission reduction targets in line with the Paris Agreement.

While shareholder proposals often demand relatively short-term action from management such as developing a strategy, they may also propose amendments to a company's articles of association that have longer-term consequences. Meaningfully diverting a company from a profit-making goal would, nevertheless, create a number of challenges. That is why some jurisdictions offer a legal structure that enables for-profit corporations to adopt objectives other than simply maximising long-term profits. This is the case of the public benefit corporations (PBC) in Delaware (currently, there are 207 private and seven listed PBCs) and sociétés à mission in France (203 private and three listed).

In some cases, shareholders and stakeholders may decide a lawsuit is the best or only solution to a disagreement with a company's management. Corporations are defendants in at least 18 climate-related court cases filed globally between May 2020 and May 2021. Climate-related corporate litigation has been traditionally focused on major carbon emitters, but an increasing number of claims cover the current fulfilment of fiduciary duties and due diligence obligations by companies and their directors in industries other than oil and gas, and cement.

# Acronyms and abbreviations

| | | | |
|---|---|---|---|
| ACSI | Australian Council of Superannuation Investors | ILO | International Labour Organization |
| AICPA | American Institute of Certified Public Accountants | IPCC | Intergovernmental Panel on Climate Change |
| BCB | Central Bank of Brazil | IPO | initial public offerings |
| BRSR | Business Responsibility and Sustainability Report | JFSA | Financial Services Agency of Japan |
| CBI | Climate Bonds Initiative | LSE | London School of Economics |
| CDP | Carbon Disclosure Project | MNE | Multinational Enterprise |
| CDSB | Climate Disclosure Standards Boards | NFRD | Non-Financial Reporting Directive |
| CMF | Financial Market Commission of Chile | NGFS | Network of Central Banks and Supervisors for Greening the Financial System |
| CSRC | Securities Regulatory Commission of China | OECD | Organisation for Economic Co-operation and Development |
| CSRD | Corporate Sustainability Reporting Directive | OJK | Financial Services Authority of Indonesia |
| CVM | Securities and Exchange Commission of Brazil | PBC | public benefit corporation |
| EU | European Union | R&D | research and development |
| EFRAG | European Financial Reporting Advisory Group | RBC | responsible business conduc |
| ESG | environmental, social and governance | ROA | return on assets |
| FASB | Financial Accounting Standards Board | ROE | return on equity |
| FCA | Financial Conduct Authority of UK | REIT | Real Estate Investment Trust |
| FSB | Financial Stability Board | SASB | Sustainability Accounting Standards Board |
| GHG | Greenhouse Gases | SBTi | Science Based Targets initiative |
| GIIN | Global Impact Investing Network | SEBI | Securities and Exchange Board of India |
| GSI | Global Sustainability Initiative | SEC | Securities and Exchange Commission of the United States |
| GSSB | Global Sustainability Standards Board | SGX | Singapore Exchange |
| HKEX | Hong Kong Exchanges and Clearing Limited | SME | Small and medium-sized enterprise |
| IAASB | International Auditing and Assurance Standards Board | STF | IOSCO's Sustainable Finance Task Force |
| IASB | International Accounting Standards Board | TCFD | Task Force on Climate-related Financial Disclosures |
| IEA | International Energy Agency | TSVCM | Taskforce on Scaling Voluntary Carbon Markets |
| IFRS | International Accounting Standards Board | UN | United Nations |
| IOSCO | International Organization of Securities Commissions | VRF | Value Reporting Foundation |
| IR | Integrated Reporting | WEF | World Economic Forum |
| ISSB | International Sustainability Standards Board | | |

# 1 Trends

This chapter describes trends in assets under management by investors considering sustainability in portfolio selection, as well as asset manager sustainability-related engagement preferences. The chapter summarises the most commonly used sustainability reporting standards and presents their use by listed companies, including whether disclosed information is assured by a third party. It then analyses the market value of companies in industries where climate change is financially material. In addition, the chapter gives an overview of how the purpose of the corporation has been understood and the definition of directors' fiduciary duties in selected jurisdictions. Finally it reviews how shareholders and stakeholders have been influencing management to incorporate climate-related matters into their decision-making processes.

## 1.1. Climate change and the Paris Agreement

Copious scientific evidence points to the fact that human-generated emissions of greenhouse gases (GHG) such as $CO_2$ and methane have caused approximately 1.0°C of global warming above pre-industrial levels (IPCC, 2021[1]). Moreover, research demonstrates that global warming is associated with more frequent flooding, loss of biodiversity, heat-related mortality, among other risks to human life, the environment and the economy. These risks are considered moderate or high in a scenario where global warming is 1.5°C above pre-industrial levels, which would mean that some adaptation in our societies, infrastructure and industrial systems would be needed to cope with global warming. However, risks become high or very high for average temperatures of 2°C or higher above pre-industrial levels, which would inflict severe impact on our societies with limited capacity to adapt (IPCC, 2018[2]). This is why 192 governments agreed to hold global warming to "well below 2°C above pre-industrial levels and to pursue efforts to limit the temperature increase to 1.5°C above pre-industrial levels" (UN, 2015, p. 3[3]), in what is known as the "Paris Agreement".

To limit global warming to 1.5°C above pre-industrial levels would effectively require $CO_2$ emissions to decline by about 45% from 2010 levels by 2030 and reach net zero emissions around 2050 (IPCC, 2018[2]). The "net zero" means that $CO_2$ emissions would still exist at low levels (including natural sources of $CO_2$), but they would be compensated by the removal and storage of $CO_2$ from the atmosphere (in this scenario, non-$CO_2$ GHG emissions would be reduced but they would not reach zero globally). So far, 165 jurisdictions have presented a national plan on how they will reduce GHG emissions in line with the Paris Agreement (so-called "nationally determined contributions"), but their planned combined emissions reductions by 2030 still fall short of the level needed to limit global warming to 1.5°C above pre-industrial levels (UN, 2021[4]). In particular, the total level of global GHG emissions in the existing nationally determined contributions of Parties to the Paris Agreement is projected to be 15.9% higher in 2030 than in 2010 and 4.7% higher than in 2019 (UN, 2021[5]).

During COP26 in November 2021, governments agreed on the Glasgow Climate Pact to accelerate action on coal, deforestation, electric vehicles and methane, and they finalised the outstanding elements of the Paris Agreement, including the establishment of a new mechanism and standards for international carbon markets (UN, 2021[6]). In the Glasgow Climate Pact, governments agreed to revisit and strengthen their current GHG emissions targets to 2030 in 2022, instead of waiting another 5-year period as established by the Paris Agreement. Likewise, 190 countries agreed to phase down unabated coal power, 137 countries committed to halt and reverse forest loss and land degradation by 2030, and over 100 countries pledged to reduce methane emissions by 30% by 2030.

There are many different pathways to net zero $CO_2$ emissions by 2050, and a great number of possible energy and environmental policies to support them. These might include, for instance, mandating the phase-out of coal-fired power stations, subsidies to renewable energy, financing technology innovation and emission trading systems for major polluters. A discussion of the advantages and drawbacks of each of those policies is outside of the scope of this report, but, as an example of the economic changes that lie ahead, the following are some of the transformations included in a global pathway to net zero emissions by 2050 set by the International Energy Agency (IEA, 2021[7]):

- annual additions of 630 GW of solar photovoltaics and 390 GW of wind by 2030 (four times the record levels in 2020)
- electric vehicles would represent more than 60% of car sales by 2030 (currently, they have a market-share of around 5%)
- in 2050, almost half the GHG emissions reduction will come from technologies that are currently at the demonstration or prototype phase, including innovation related to batteries, hydrogen, and $CO_2$ capture and storage
- fossil fuels decline from almost four-fifths of total energy supply today to slightly over one-fifth by 2050
- 90% of heavy industrial production becomes low-emissions by 2050, including with the use of hydrogen and $CO_2$ capture technologies.

The Paris Agreement also sets out that implementation will require economic and social transformation based on the best available science. The preamble to the Paris Agreement reflects the close links between climate action, sustainable development, and a just transition, with Parties "taking into account the imperatives of a just transition of the workforce and the creation of decent work and quality jobs in accordance with nationally defined development priorities" (UN, 2015, p. 2[3]).

## 1.2. Investors' perspective

Asset owners such as pension funds and families have taken notice of the risks and opportunities that climate change and an expected transition to net zero emissions by 2050 (among other environmental and social trends) might represent for their investee assets. Consequently, the total assets under management by professional investors that consider ESG risk factors in portfolio selection and management has grown significantly. While the definition of sustainable investment varies between countries and over time, Table 1.1 and Figure 1.1 provide an indicative snapshot of the growing global importance of sustainable investing assets.[1]

### Table 1.1. Snapshot of global sustainable investing assets

In USD billions

| | 2016 | 2018 | 2020 |
|---|---|---|---|
| United States | 8 723 | 11 995 | 17 081 |
| Europe | 12 040 | 14 075 | 12 017 |
| Japan | 474 | 2 180 | 2 874 |
| Canada | 1 086 | 1 699 | 2 423 |
| Australia and New Zealand | 516 | 734 | 906 |
| **Total** | **22 839** | **30 683** | **35 301** |

Note: Significant changes in the way sustainable investment is defined have been adopted in Australia, Europe and New Zealand, so direct comparisons across regions and time are not easily made.
Source: GSI Alliance (2021[8]), *Global Sustainable Investment Review 2020*, http://www.gsi-alliance.org/.

### Figure 1.1. Proportion of sustainable investing assets relative to total managed assets

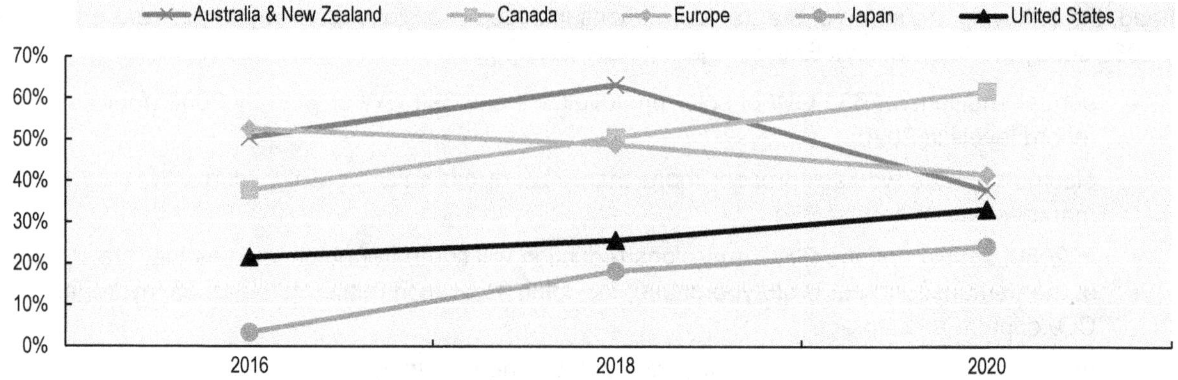


Note: Significant changes in the way sustainable investment is defined have been adopted in Australia, Europe and New Zealand, so direct comparisons between regions and years are not easily made.
Source: GSI Alliance (2021[8]), *GSI Alliance, Global Sustainable Investment Alliance*, http://www.gsi-alliance.org/.

Since most of the sustainable investing data rely on survey-based approaches, the large numbers above should be taken with caution because part of the value of sustainable investing assets may be attributed to asset managers who claim to adopt sustainable or ESG-conscious strategies but who do not necessarily contribute to more social and environmental sustainability. This could be either due to misleading investors when labelling a financial product (including so-called "greenwashing") or because the mandated goals of an investor are not aligned with what the best scientific evidence would recommend. One clear conclusion can be extracted from the numbers above: asset owners such as pension funds and households in Canada, the United States and Japan have increasingly allocated their portfolios to investment vehicles that purport to be sustainable. In Europe, Australia and New Zealand, it is difficult to draw any conclusion on trends between 2016 and 2020 because of changes in the definition of sustainable investment during that period, but the proportion of sustainable investing assets relative to total managed assets in 2020 was high (above 37%) (GSI Alliance, 2021[8]).

A relatively small subset of the sustainable investing universe is composed of investment funds that label themselves as ESG or sustainable funds – for instance by including "ESG" or "sustainable investing" terms in their names. Focussing only on investment funds, and using a different database than in Table 1.1, shows a strong growth in assets under management for these ESG funds[2], which reached USD 1.7 trillion in 2021 (Figure 1.2). This was mainly the result of record net inflow amounts in 2020 and 2021 with USD 241 billion and USD 586 billion, respectively. While the value of assets under management by climate funds was very modest between 2016 and 2019, net inflows in 2020 and 2021 were 6 and 19 times that of the previous three year average (2017-19), respectively.

Figure 1.2. Assets under management of funds labelled as or focusing on ESG and climate

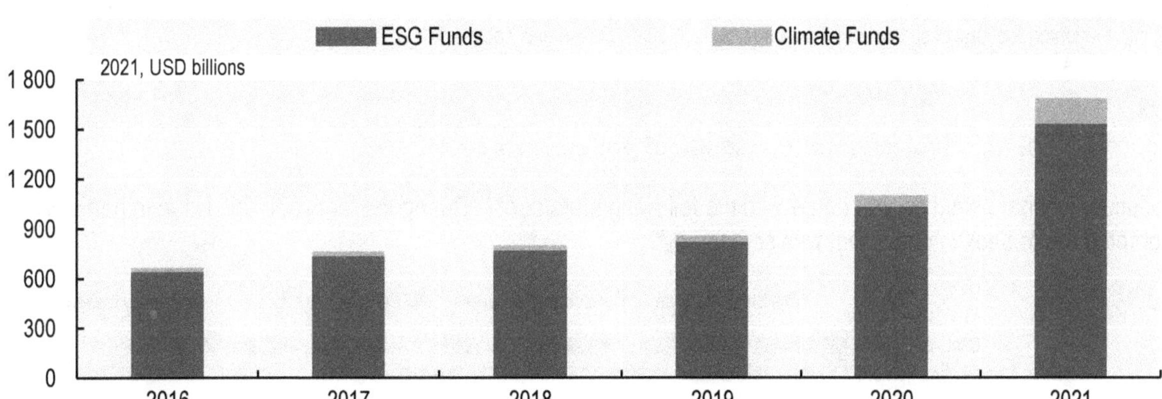


Note: Funds retrieved from Reuters Funds Screen classified as Climate Funds or ESG Funds in the case their names contain, respectively, climate or ESG relevant acronyms and words such as ESG, sustainable, responsible, ethical, green and climate (and their translation in other languages). Funds without any asset value are excluded.
Source: Thomson Reuters Eikon, Datastream, OECD calculations.

While the numbers in Table 1.2 involve the same challenges of categorisation previously mentioned, the following features of the current sustainable investing universe can still be identified:

- the most significant strategy (with USD 25 trillion) is the integration by asset managers of ESG factors into their financial analysis;
- strategies that often accept a tangible trade-off between wealth creation and better ESG results ("Impact/community investing") currently amount to USD 352 billion[3] (only 1.4% when compared to the "ESG integration" strategy);
- assets under management by investors who claim to employ shareholder power to influence corporate behaviour on ESG-related issues has reached a meaningful value of USD 10.5 trillion.[4]

As acknowledged at the outset of this section, sustainable investing is a wide category that encompasses ESG issues of very different nature, from climate change to human rights. Figure 1.3 shows the current engagement preferences of a sample of institutional investors (investors not necessarily self-reported as "sustainable investors" with USD 29 trillion in assets under management). The sample (with some overrepresentation of UK-based investors) shows clearly that climate change and associated risks are the number one priority with respect to engagement with companies, followed by human capital management (a social issue), board composition and executive remuneration (governance issues).

### Table 1.2. Sustainable investing assets by strategy in 2020

| Sustainable investment strategy | Definition | Assets (USD billions) |
|---|---|---|
| ESG integration | The systematic and explicit inclusion by investment managers of ESG factors into financial analysis. | 25 195 |
| Negative screening | The exclusion from a portfolio of certain sectors, companies, countries or other issuers based on activities considered not investable (e.g. excluding tobacco companies). | 15 030 |
| Corporate engagement and shareholder action | Employing shareholder power to influence corporate behaviour, including through proxy voting that is guided by comprehensive ESG guidelines. | 10 504 |
| Norm-based screening | Screening of investments against minimum standards of business practice based on international norms such as those issued by the UN, ILO and OECD. | 4 140 |
| Sustainability-themed investing | Investing in themes or assets specifically contributing to sustainable solutions (e.g. sustainable agriculture and gender equity). | 1 948 |
| Best-in-class screening | Investment in sectors or companies selected for positive ESG performance relative to industry peers, and that achieve a rating above a defined threshold. | 1 384 |
| Impact/community investing | Investing to achieve positive social and environmental impact. | 352 |

Note: Asset managers may apply more than one strategy to a given pool of assets, so there is double-counting if one adds all strategies above. For information on the total of sustainable investing assets in 2020, please see Table 1.1.
Source: GSI Alliance (2021[8]), *Global Sustainable Investment Review 2020*, http://www.gsi-alliance.org/.

### Figure 1.3. Institutional investor engagement preferences in 2020

Question: to what extent do you agree with the following statement? “During the last year, this issue in particular has prompted me to seek engagement with companies”

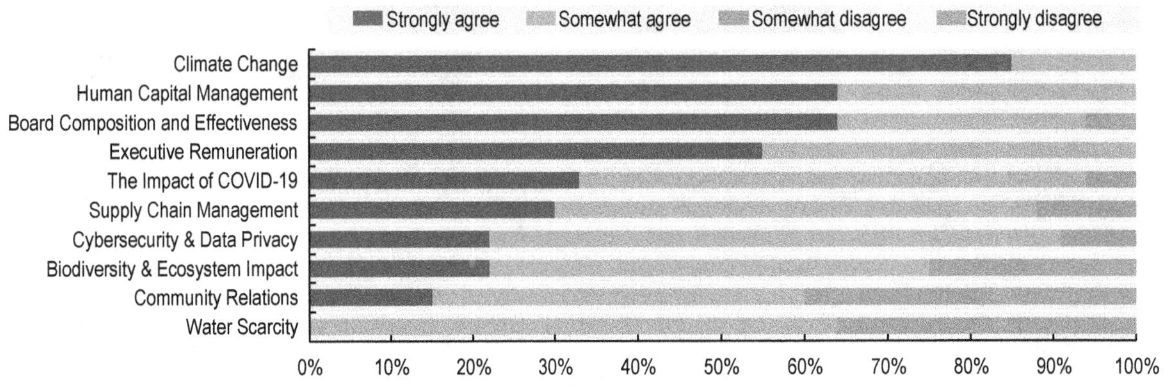


Note: 42 global institutional investors (not necessarily self-reported as "sustainable investors") with USD 29 trillion in assets under management (with nearly two-thirds of their portfolio in equity) participated in the survey. The geographical distribution of those investors was the following: UK (33%); the United States (17%); Europe excl-UK (12%); rest of the world (38%).
Source: Morrow Sodali (2021[9]), *Institutional Investor Survey 2021*, https://morrowsodali.com/insights/institutional-investor-survey-2021.

## 1.3. Financial stability

Financial stability supervisors currently also have climate change at the top of their sustainability agenda, since a great number of firms may become unable to pay their debt or their assets may quickly lose value depending on the consequences of climate change on their businesses and management's capacity to grapple with climate-related risks. Climate-related risks are usually classified under two categories (TCFD, 2017, p. 62[10]): (i) physical risks, which result either from extreme weather events or long-term shifts in climate patterns (e.g. flooding and higher temperatures); (ii) transition risks, which are associated with changes in public policies, legal actions, a shift to low-carbon technologies, market responses to climate change and reputational considerations (e.g. carbon pricing policies and decrease in the sales of internal combustion engine vehicles).

The FSB, within its mandate to promote international financial stability, has been leading work on how climate-related risks might impact the financial system. One of the most consequential outcomes of the FSB's work was the establishment in 2015 of an industry-led Task Force on Climate-related Financial Disclosures (TCFD). The initial goal of the TCFD was to develop a set of voluntary disclosure recommendations for use by companies in providing decision-useful information to investors, lenders and insurance underwriters about the climate-related financial risks that companies face (the main recommendations issued in 2017 are summarised below).

Another initiative, among many others, is the Network of Central Banks and Supervisors for Greening the Financial System (NGFS), which brings together 114 institutions and whose purpose is to contribute to the development of climate- and environment-related risk management and mobilise mainstream finance to support the transition toward a sustainable economy. NGFS member jurisdictions cover more than 2/3 of the global systemically important banks and insurers. In 2019, the NGFS issued six recommendations to financial supervisors and relevant stakeholders to foster a greener financial system, including one related to "achieving robust and internationally consistent climate and environment-related disclosure" (NGFS, 2019[11]).

## 1.4. Reporting frameworks and standards

Today, companies use a great number of frameworks and standards to disclose information on their climate-related and other ESG performance, risks and strategy. Table 1.3 summarises the most frequently used frameworks and standards[5] with respect to how detailed they are, their targeted audience, the issues they cover and the threshold they recommend for information to be disclosed (i.e. which issues would be material for the framework). Possible definitions of "materiality" are discussed in more detail further below, but, concisely, corporate disclosure is "financially material" if it could reasonably be expected to influence an investor or a lender's analysis of a company's future cash flows. A "double materiality" concept incorporates what is financially material, but it also includes within its scope information that would be relevant to the understanding of multiple stakeholders of a company's effect on the environment, on people or on society (e.g. for consumers and employees).

### Table 1.3. Climate-related and other ESG reporting frameworks and standards

| Institution | System | Level of detail | Materiality | Audience | Issues |
|---|---|---|---|---|---|
| FSB's TCFD | TCFD recommendations | Principles-based[1] | Financially material | Investors, lenders and insurance underwriters | Climate-related issues |
| IFRS Foundation – International Sustainability Standards Board (ISSB)2 | IFRS Sustainability Standards[2] | Detailed information | Financially material | Investors | Initial focus on climate-related issues, but with a plan to cover a great number of ESG issues |
| Value Reporting Foundation – SASB Standards Board3 | SASB Standards | Detailed information | Financially material | Investors | A great number of ESG issues, with subset of standards in each of 77 industries |
| Value Reporting Foundation – Integrated Reporting Framework Board3 | <IR> Framework | Principles-based | Financially material | Investors | A great number of ESG issues |

| Institution | System | Level of detail | Materiality | Audience | Issues |
|---|---|---|---|---|---|
| Global Sustainability Standards Board (GSSB) | GRI Standards | Detailed information | Double materiality | Multiple stakeholders | A great number of ESG issues, with a plan to have a subset of standards in each of 40 sectors |
| GHG Protocol | GHG Protocol Corporate Standards | Detailed information | -[4] | -[4] | GHG emissions[4] |
| CDP (previously "Carbon Disclosure Project") | CDP's questionnaires[5] | Detailed information | -[5] | Investors and customers | Climate change, forests and water security[5] |
| Climate Disclosure Standards Board (CDSB)6 | CDSB Framework | Principles-based | Financially material and relevant[7] | Investors | Climate and other environmental information |

Notes:

1: While TCFD's recommendations (TCFD, 2017[10]) are indeed principles-based, the Task Force has published a number of documents providing detailed guidance on how to better comply with its recommendations, such as the report "Guidance on Scenario Analysis for Non-Financial Companies" (TCFD, 2020[12]). To some extent, therefore, this set of recommendations and guidance documents on how companies may disclose financially material information, preferably in mainstream financial filings, would together demand "detailed information" according to the classification in the third column of this table.

2: IFRS Foundation announced in November 2021 the formation of the International Sustainability Standards Board (ISSB), which will sit alongside the International Accounting Standards Board (IASB), to set IFRS Sustainability Disclosure Standards. As a part of this, IFRS Foundation committed to consolidate with the Value Reporting Foundation Board and CDSB by June 2022. IFRS Foundation's recently amended constitution provides that IFRS Sustainability Disclosure Standards "are intended to result in the provision of high-quality, transparent and comparable information [...] in sustainability disclosures that is useful to investors and other participants in the world's capital markets in making economic decisions" (item 2.a). Please see section 2.4 on ISSB's goals and planned work.

3: SASB Standards Board and Integrated Reporting Framework Board (<IR> Framework Board) merged in June 2021. Currently, both standard-setting boards are supervised by a newly created organisation called Value Reporting Foundation Board (VRF). In November 2021, the VRF committed to consolidate into the recently created ISSB by June 2022.

4: GHG Protocol's corporate accounting and reporting standard provides requirements and guidance for companies preparing a corporate-level GHG emissions inventory. It does not adopt a materiality concept, and other ESG reporting frameworks and standards will typically either require or allow GHG emissions to be disclosed according to GHG Protocol's standard. In this standard, GHG emissions are classified under three categories: Scope 1 (direct emissions from a company's own operations); Scope 2 (emissions from purchased or acquired electricity, steam, heat and cooling); Scope 3 (the entire chain of emissions impact from the goods the company purchases to the products it sells).

5: CDP's questionnaires would not be considered a reporting framework or standard in the traditional sense, but the institution offers a widely used system for companies to answer to any of the following questionnaires: Climate Change; Forests; Water Security. The questionnaires are meant to be disclosed to (i) investors or to (ii) customers interested in assessing the environmental impact of their supply-chain. Corporate management is not supposed to make a materiality assessment of the information to disclose, because CDP offers a set of questions by economic sector and companies have strong incentives to answer all of them in order to receive better scores calculated by CDP's system. Questionnaires are shortened only for companies with an annual revenue of less than EUR/USD 250 million and corporates answering the questionnaire for the first time.

6: In January 2022, the CDSB consolidated into the IFRS Foundation.

7: According to the CDSB Framework, environmental information should be disclosed if financially material or relevant. "Relevant" in this context would be information that might be financially material at some point, while the link between the information and future cash flows is not evident. In either case, GHG emissions shall be reported in all cases regardless of management's assessment of their materiality or relevance (CDSB, 2019[13]).

Source: Standards, frameworks and websites of the institutions visited in July and November 2021 and January 2022; OECD elaboration.

For a company that is choosing which reporting framework to use or for a regulator that is considering whether to recommend or require a particular framework, a first question could be which broad issues are the most relevant to the company and to the market (last column in Table 1.3). For instance, TCFD recommendations cover climate-related risks only, while the SASB Board and GSSB offer reporting standards on a full breadth of ESG issues. Therefore, for example, if climate-related risks are the most material risks in a specific context, compliance with the TCFD recommendations might be more relevant to initially focus on, before considering whether to report on other environmental and social dimensions, using SASB or GRI reporting standards for instance.

Another question for companies and regulators assessing existing ESG reporting frameworks is who would be the primary users of the information to be disclosed (the fifth column in Table 1.3). A large majority of existing ESG reporting frameworks cite investors in equity and debt as their main audience with the notable exceptions of the GRI Standards, which aim at being used by shareholders and multiple stakeholders, and CDP's questionnaires, which have both investors and supply chain customers as their audience. A focus on the information needs of existing and potential investors and lenders has been traditionally adopted by financial reporting standards (IASB, 2018[14]). However, as important as the definition of the main audience of the disclosure may be, the disclosed information might still be relevant to users that are not considered primary. For instance, $CO_2$ emissions will likely be relevant to shareholders of an oil and gas company as primary users due to the potential cash flow impact of carbon pricing policies in the future, but it may also be of interest to consumers or environmentally conscious employees who would prefer to work in a low-carbon company.

The definition of materiality in an ESG disclosure framework or standard goes largely hand in hand with the profile of its primary users (fourth column in Table 1.3). If the primary users are investors, it is often assumed that they make investment and voting decisions mostly based on a company's expected future cash flows and their timing. Only the CDSB Framework – which focuses only on environmental and climate change information and considers investors as the primary users – somewhat diverges from this general rule in two ways: (i) by requiring disclosure of information even if its impact on a company's cash flows is not evident but could become relevant; (ii) by mandating transparency of GHG emissions in all cases regardless of management's assessment of its materiality.

ESG reporting frameworks and standards summarised in Table 1.3 also vary with respect to the level of detail of their guidance and requirements (see third column). Some of them are principles-based, which allows for flexibility when implemented by companies with different characteristics and operating in different countries. Flexibility, however, makes consistency across time and comparability between companies more difficult, which is why some ESG reporting standards provide greater detail on how companies should account and report on sustainability information.

Two additional features of ESG reporting should be highlighted. First, companies may choose to report sustainability information based on two different standards with similar coverage of issues, as long as they clearly segment the disclosed information (for instance, according to SASB for investors and GRI standards for a wider public). Second, a principles-based framework may serve as the overall guidance to management when reporting sustainability information according to a more detailed standard (for instance, using the <IR> Framework when developing a sustainability report with information required by SASB Standards).

TCFD recommendations receive particular attention in this report because of their focus on climate-related risks. The Task Force's recommendations suggest the disclosure of financially material information, preferably in mainstream financial filings, around four thematic areas (TCFD, 2017[10]):

- Governance – the organisation's governance around climate-related risks and opportunities
- Strategy – the actual and potential impacts of climate-related risks and opportunities on the organisation's businesses, strategy and financial planning. This would include impact analysis of different climate-related scenarios, including a 2ºC or lower scenario in line with the Paris Agreement
- Risk management – the processes used by the organisation to identify, assess and manage climate-related risks
- Metrics and targets – the metrics and targets used to assess and manage relevant climate-related risks and opportunities, including greenhouse gas emissions.

While TCFD recommendations are principles-based, the Task Force has published a number of documents providing detailed guidance on how to better comply with its recommendations, such as the report "Guidance on Scenario Analysis for Non-Financial Companies" (TCFD, 2020[12]). To some extent, therefore, these recommendations and guidance would together demand "detailed information" according to the classification in the third column of Table 1.3.

TCFD analysis of the implementation of its standard shows uneven progress to date. Its 2021 analysis of 1 651 public companies from 69 countries across eight industries particularly exposed to climate-related risks[6] over the previous three years assessed whether their reports included information that appeared to align with the Task Force's 11 recommended disclosures, which are organised around the four thematic areas mentioned above (TCFD, 2021, pp. 28, 30[15]). Despite some recent progress, the conclusion of the analysis is that only 50% of companies reviewed disclosed information in alignment with at least three recommended disclosures. The information item most often disclosed by companies was "climate-related risks and opportunities" (52% of companies in 2020) and the least disclosed item was "resilience of strategies under different climate-related scenarios" (13% of companies in 2020). Among the four thematic areas, "governance" is the one with the smallest uptake: its two recommended disclosures are the second and third least disclosed. In 2020, Europe remained the leading region for TCFD-aligned disclosures (a company headquartered in Europe disclosed on average 50% of the 11 recommended disclosures), while the disclosure rate was 34% in the Asia Pacific, 26% in Latin America, 22% in the Middle East and Africa, and 20% in North America (TCFD, 2021, p. 34[15]).[7]

The multitude of existing standards and frameworks (seven in Table 1.3) raises the question of whether climate-related information is comparable between companies that effectively disclose them. Figure 1.4 presents the use of four abovementioned ESG standards and frameworks by S&P 500 companies that published a sustainability report in 2019 (90% of the large-cap index companies published such a report).

Figure 1.4. Use of ESG reporting standards by S&P 500 companies in 2019

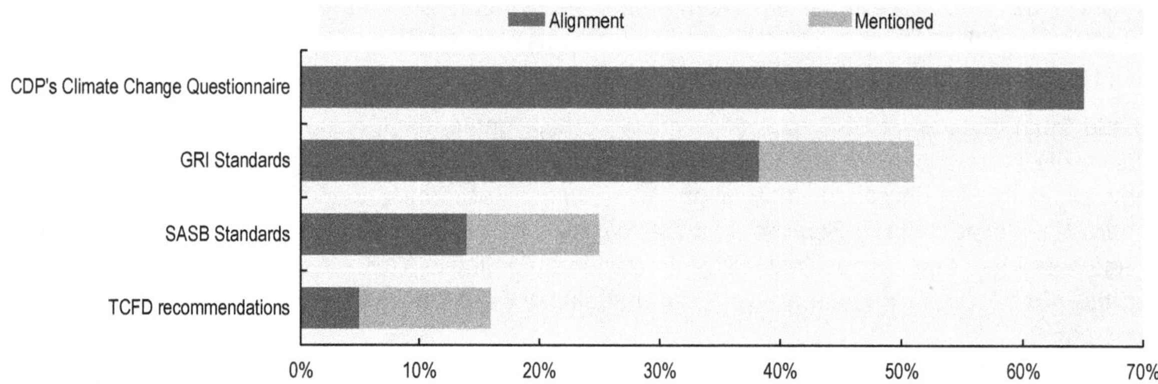


Notes:
1: Use of ESG reporting standards and frameworks was classified in the analysis as purported "alignment" with the standard or simply as having "mentioned" the standard in the sustainability report.
2: Some sustainability reports from S&P 500 companies followed or mentioned more than one ESG reporting standard in their sustainability report. This is the reason why the percentages in this graph add up to more than 100%.
Source: G&A Institute (2020[16]), *Trends on the sustainability reporting practices of S&P Index companies*, https://www.ga-institute.com/research-reports/flash-reports/2020-sp-500-flash-report.html.

Conscious of the challenges posed by a multiplicity of ESG frameworks and standards, a majority of the institutions listed in Table 1.3 (SASB Standards Board, GSSB, <IR> Framework Board, CDSB and CDP) initiated in 2018 a project to achieve the highest possible alignment between their frameworks and standards with respect to climate-related reporting, while recognising that those institutions may have different objectives (Corporate Reporting Dialogue, 2019[17]). The same group of institutions also published in 2020 a prototype for climate-related financial disclosures building on their own reporting systems and TCFD recommendations, which is intended to be a starting point for the development of a harmonised global standard (2020[18]). While overlaps and conflicting requirements between ESG reporting standards and frameworks are not assessed in this report, Figure 1.5 shows that investors do have clear preferences for some ESG standards, which may suggest that existing standards are indeed significantly different.

### Figure 1.5. Institutional investor ESG reporting preferences in 2020

Question: What is your preferred ESG framework for companies to best disclose their material ESG topics?

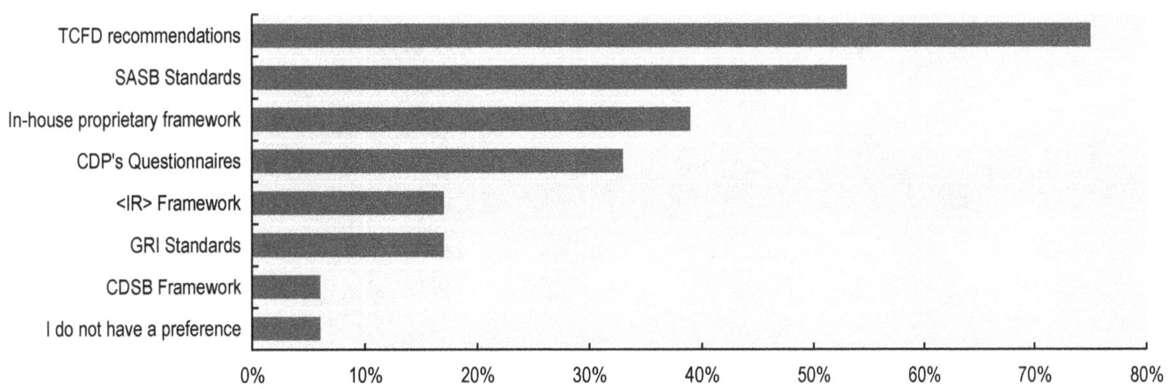


Notes:
1: For information on respondents to the survey, see notes to Figure 1.3.
2: Respondents to the survey could choose more than one preferred ESG framework, what explains why the numbers in this figure add up to more than 100%. Specifically, the survey found that a number of institutional investors, including BlackRock, State Street Global Advisors and Vanguard, have called out TCFD recommendations and SASB Standards as the two ESG frameworks that listed companies should follow.
Source: Morrow Sodali (2021[9]), *Institutional Investor Survey 2021*, https://morrowsodali.com/insights/institutional-investor-survey-2021.

The use of multiple sustainability-related and ESG reporting standards and frameworks is not, however, the only barrier to greater consistency and comparability of corporate sustainability disclosure. If disclosed ESG information is not assured by a third-party based on robust methodologies (as financial reports of listed companies must typically be), it could undermine confidence in the information disclosed and the possibility to compare sustainability reports between companies. In 2019, only 29% of S&P 500 companies that reported on sustainability sought external assurance.[8] Moreover, just 5% of those assurances were in relation to the entire sustainability report and in 40% of cases they certified only information on GHG emissions (G&A Institute, 2020[16]).

A global analysis of 1 400 large listed companies in 22 major jurisdictions[9] found that 91% of companies reported some level of sustainability information, and that 51% of those that disclosed sustainability information in 2019 provided some level of assurance by a third party (44% for those based outside the EU). Eighty-three percent of these assurance engagements, however, resulted in only "limited" assurance reports. The remaining small minority offered a higher level of "moderate" or "reasonable" assurances (IFAC and AICPA, 2021[19]).

## 1.5. Companies' perspective

Another important consideration is the number and market value of public companies in industries where either GHG emissions or the physical impacts of climate change are indeed financially material. One way of evaluating this is to identify listed companies that operate in industries where GHG emissions, energy management and the physical impacts of climate change are considered to be financially material according to the SASB Sustainable Industry Classification System® Taxonomy (SASB mapping),[10] which is set by the SASB Board through a process of research and public consultation.[11]

In the SASB mapping, 51 out of 77 industries are considered to face financially material risks related to Scopes 1 and 2 GHG emissions[12] (in the classification used in Table 1.4, "energy management" is closely related to GHG Scope 2 emission risks) as well as the physical impacts of climate change. The number of companies and their market capitalisation in those 51 industries (11 sectors encompass all those industries) are presented in Table 1.4.[13]

### Table 1.4. Companies in sectors where GHG emissions, energy management and physical impacts of climate change are likely to be financially material in 2021

| Sector | Number of companies | Market capitalisation (USD billion) |
|---|---|---|
| Technology & Communications | 3 735 | 24 782 |
| Resource Transformation | 5 637 | 11 732 |
| Extractives & Minerals Processing | 3 859 | 9 934 |
| Transportation | 1 634 | 9 326 |
| Food & Beverage | 2 696 | 6 756 |
| Consumer Goods | 1 967 | 6 683 |
| Infrastructure | 2 365 | 5 031 |
| Financials | 722 | 3 758 |
| Health Care | 585 | 2 028 |
| Services | 751 | 933 |
| Renewable Resources & Alternative Energy | 406 | 914 |
| **Total** | **24 357** | **81 878** |

Notes:
1: Sector classification is according to SASB mapping.
2: According to the SASB mapping, Physical Impacts of Climate Change is classified under the dimension of "Business Model & Innovation".
Source: OECD Capital Market Series Dataset, Factset, Thomson Reuters Eikon, Bloomberg, SASB mapping and OECD calculations.

### Table 1.5. Share of market capitalisation where selected risks are likely to be financially material by sustainability issues in 2021

| **Sustainability Issues** | **Share of market capitalisation of industries where the risk is material (in total global market cap.)** | **Number of industries where the risk is material (out of a total of 77)** |
|---|---|---|
| Energy Management | 47% | 33 |
| GHG Emissions | 27% | 25 |
| Water & Wastewater Management | 26% | 25 |
| Waste & Hazardous Materials Management | 21% | 19 |
| Air Quality | 15% | 17 |
| Ecological Impacts | 9% | 14 |
| Physical Impacts of Climate Change | 6% | 8 |

Note: Sector classification is according to SASB mapping.
Source: OECD Capital Market Series Dataset, Factset, Thomson Reuters Eikon, Bloomberg, SASB mapping and OECD calculations.

On top of GHG emissions, energy management and physical impacts of climate change, sustainability issues also relate to other environmental, social and governance topics.[14] In order to have a broader perspective on the risks relating to the environment, Table 1.5 presents the share of market capitalisation of companies in sectors where environmental issues are likely to be financially material as a percentage of total global market capitalisation. The table also shows the corresponding number of industries according to the SASB mapping.

According to the SASB mapping, "energy management", which is closely related to GHG Scope 2 emissions, is an environmental risk that is likely to be financially material for 33 out of 77 industries that account for half of the global market capitalisation in 2021. In addition, 25 industries that represent a quarter of the global market capitalisation are associated with GHG emissions (Scope 1) risks. On top of that, 6% of the global market capitalisation across eight industries are materially exposed to the physical impacts of climate change. Taking these three risks together, climate change is considered to be a financially material risk for listed companies that account for 65% of the global market capitalisation of all listed companies today.

Table 1.5 cannot be read as the market value adjusted for specific risks, which would depend on an individual assessment of each company's financial exposure to these risks. For instance, a company with a sound strategy to navigate the transition to a low-carbon economy may face low risks despite the fact it is in a high climate-related financial risk industry such as metals and mining. However, in the absence of disclosure of comparable value-at-risk information by a representative sample of companies, the share of market capitalisation in Table 1.5 and in Figure 1.6 can serve as a reference to policy makers on how differences in economic sectors' distribution among local listed companies may justify distinct priorities when supervising and regulating their capital markets.

In line with the global distribution of companies in terms of environmental risks, companies in sectors where energy management (Scope 2) is considered a financially material risk have the highest share of market capitalisation across jurisdictions (Figure 1.6) – in particular, more than 50% of the market capitalisation of the US, Japanese and Chinese markets. In absolute terms, the US listed corporate sector is also highly exposed to the rest of the selected sustainability risks, while their share by market capitalisation is among the lowest in comparison to other countries and regions shown in Figure 1.6. The opposite trend is true for the rest of the world: while the market capitalisation of companies in sectors likely to be exposed to the selected sustainability risks is relatively low, their share in relation to total market capitalisation is comparatively higher.

### Figure 1.6. The share of market capitalisation by selected risks, 2021

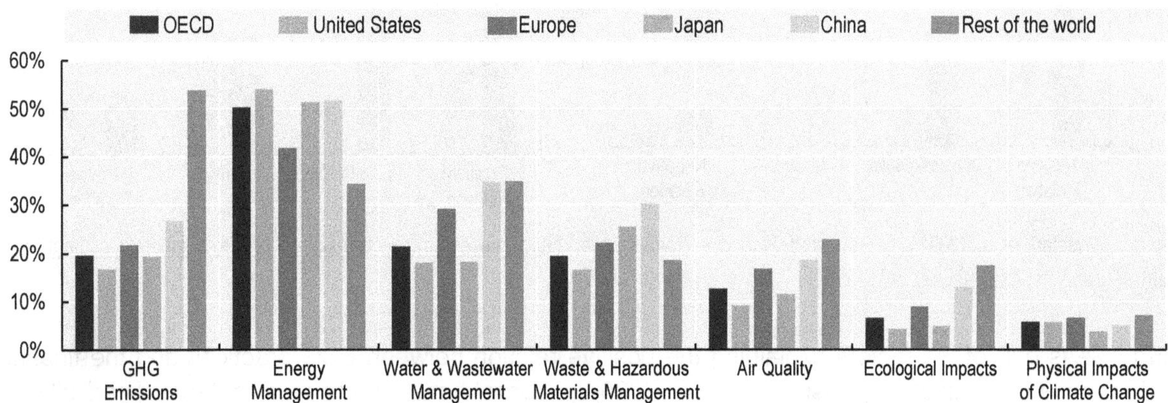


Source: OECD Capital Market Series Dataset, Factset, Thomson Reuters Eikon, Bloomberg, SASB mapping, and OECD calculations.

Another central question concerning corporate sustainability is whether better ESG practices could enhance financial performance and resilience, for instance through improved risk management and better strategy.

A large volume of research suggests that the better the level of company ESG practices, the higher their financial performance,[15] albeit with some divergence in findings. A 2021 paper published by NYU Stern Center for Sustainable Business and Rockefeller Asset Management reviewed the findings of 245 research papers issued between 2015 and 2020 (Wheelan et al.[20]). The review concludes that 58% of the papers found a positive correlation between ESG practices (such as suggested by high ESG ratings) and operational and financial metrics (such as return on equity, return on assets and stock prices). In 21% of the papers, there were mixed results (the same study found positive, neutral or negative results), 13% did not find a clear relationship and only 8% showed a negative relationship.[16]

The meta-analysis found a weaker relation between investors' focus on ESG risks and the performance of their portfolios. In reviewed studies looking from an investor's perspective, 33% showed better performance for securities portfolios with a purported focus on ESG risks taking into account their risk-adjusted returns (such as a Sharpe ratio), in 28% the results were mixed, in 26% a clear relationship was not identified and 14% found negative results.

It is important to note that many of the studies reviewed faced methodological challenges such as the low standardisation of ESG data and lack of emphasis of some investment vehicles on financially material issues, which may limit the conclusiveness of their results (Wheelan et al., 2021[20]). Moreover, some other empirical evidence suggests that better financial and investment performance is also correlated with the governance aspect specifically – the G in ESG, company fundamentals, and the size and geographical location of the company (S&P Global, 2019[21]; Belsom and Lake, 2021[22]; Ratsimiveh et al., 2020[23]; Boffo and Patalano, 2020[24]).

## Figure 1.7. Studies focussing on the relation between ESG and performance

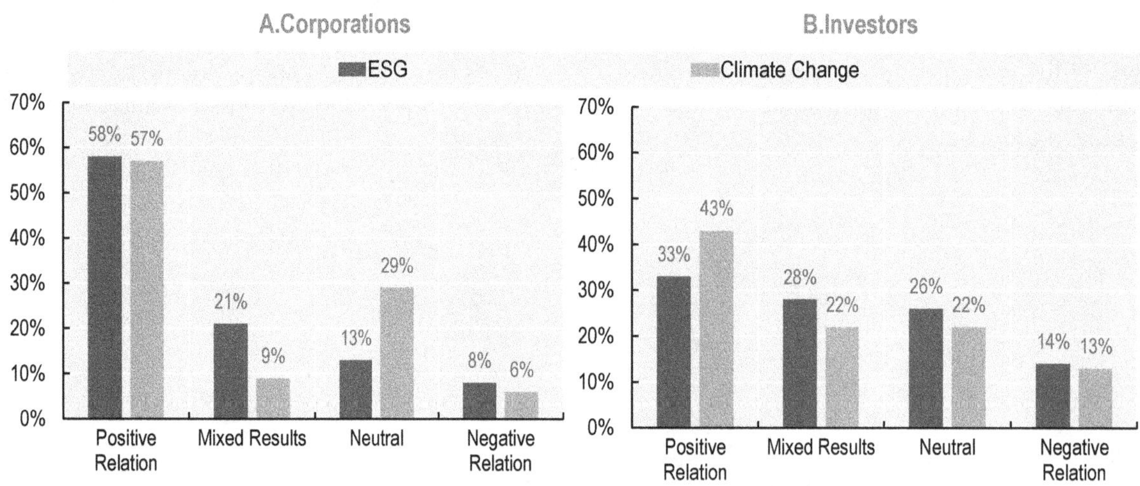


Source: Wheelan et al. (2021[20]), *ESG and Financial Performance*, https://www.stern.nyu.edu/sites/default/files/assets/documents/NYU-RAM_ESG-Paper_2021%20Rev_0.pdf.

Firm size is one of the factors explaining the positive relation between ESG practices and the financial performance of companies (Ratsimiveh et al., 2020[23]). Larger firms tend to perform better financially, for instance due to economies of scale, and, because they have relatively more resources available, they may also adopt policies and practices that help them increase their ESG scores. Table 1.6 presents size and performance indicators of 7 801 listed companies around the world[17] that have an ESG score from Refinitiv, with the median ESG score taken as a threshold to classify companies either as low or high scoring.

### Table 1.6. Size and performance indicators for companies by ESG score

| Average of 2017-21 | Low ESG scored companies | High ESG scored companies |
|---|---|---|
| ESG Score (out of 100) | 26 | 56 |
| Market capitalisation (USD billion) | 1.2 | 4.4 |
| ROE (%) | 3.6 | 4.6 |
| ROA (%) | 8.7 | 10.6 |

Note: Companies without market capitalisation, ROE and ROA are excluded from the analysis. Indicators for each company are calculated as a 5-year average whenever available. The values presented in the table are median of the indicators within each ESG scored category. ESG Score refers to Refinitiv ESG Score retrieved from Thomson Reuters Eikon public companies data. The score is calculated based on the methodology designed by Refinitiv and defined as an overall score based on the publicly reported information in the environmental, social, and corporate governance pillars. For more information on methodology, please see here.
Source: Thomson Reuters Eikon, Datastream, OECD calculations.

As presented in Table 1.6, companies with higher ESG scores are on average larger in terms of market capitalisation than the ones with lower scores, both for the entire dataset and for individual sectors. This relation holds also with respect to performance indicators of return on equity (ROE) and return on assets (ROA) for the entire dataset, however, for some of the sectors, such as consumer non-cyclicals, financials, industrials and utilities, performance in terms of ROE does not seem to differ much between low and high ESG scored companies.

Despite some divergence in research findings about the business case for better ESG practices, companies' attention to and disclosure on sustainability issues have become increasingly visible. This can be seen not only in the high number of companies that report on sustainability (as mentioned in Section 1.4), but also in the adoption of ESG metrics in executive compensation plans. While most of the components of executive remuneration plans are still linked to financial measures, companies have begun to integrate ESG-related metrics in their plans. Globally, executive compensation plans were linked to performance measures in 90% of the 9 000 largest companies with almost USD 104.5 trillion market capitalisation[18] as of the end of 2021 (i.e. part of executives' remuneration is variable). Thirty percent of companies with performance-linked executive remuneration use ESG-linked performance measures in their plans. The data also shows a high correlation between the ESG scores of companies and the use of ESG performance measures.

### Table 1.7. Executive compensation plans with ESG performance measures in 2021

| ESG scores | Companies with policy executive compensation plans (number of companies) | | share of ESG performance measures |
|---|---|---|---|
| | with performance measures | with ESG performance measures | |
| 0-25 | 1 545 | 182 | 12% |
| 25-50 | 3 224 | 728 | 23% |
| 50-75 | 2 650 | 1 081 | 41% |
| 75-100 | 771 | 505 | 65% |
| Total | 8 190 | 2 496 | 30% |

Note: ESG Score refers to Refinitiv ESG Score retrieved from Thomson Reuters Eikon public companies data. The score is calculated based on the methodology designed by Refinitiv and defined as an overall score based on the publicly reported information in the environmental, social, and corporate governance pillars. For more information on methodology, please see here.
Source: Thomson Reuters Eikon, OECD calculations.

A more detailed analysis of company specific executive pay applications in terms of ESG metrics among FTSE 100[19] companies shows that in around 30% of companies, targets relating to long-standing ESG metrics are integrated into executives' compensation plans. Importantly, half of those ESG targets relate to risks that are not material to the company according to the risk classification of the SASB mapping. In only half of the FTSE 100 companies with ESG targets in their executives' compensation plans, output measures are in the form of quantifiable goals such as GHG emission reductions or carbon emissions targets (Gosling et al., 2021[25]). This may explain why the UK Investment Association – which represents asset managers – wrote to the FTSE 350 Remuneration Committee chairs in November 2021, setting out that ESG factors in the company's variable remuneration should be "quantifiable and clearly linked to company strategy" (The Investment Association, 2021[26]).

An additional initiative aimed at supporting companies' efforts to put climate change objectives into practice through more specific GHG emission reduction targets is the Science Based Targets initiative (SBTi), supported by the CDP, the United Nations Global Compact and others to provide guidance to companies on how to set targets in line with what the latest climate science deems necessary to meet the goals of the Paris Agreement. SBTi recommends a five-step process: the company i) submits a letter establishing its intent to set a science-based target; ii) develops an emissions reduction target in line with the SBTi's criteria; iii) presents its target to the SBTi for official validation; iv) announces the validated target to its shareholders and stakeholders; v) discloses company-wide emissions in line with the GHG Protocol guidelines and tracks target progress annually (Science Based Targets Initiative, 2021[27]).

## 1.6. A corporation's objective

A significant portion of the academic and public debate on corporations during the last 50 years has been largely based on two assumptions: (i) equity investors have the sole goal of maximising their financial returns relative to a risk they are willing to accept; (ii) companies' stakeholders and society at large should have their well-being properly considered in contracts and statutes (e.g. employment contracts and environmental laws). If these assumptions hold in reality, the maximisation of long-term shareholder value would be the optimal purpose for corporations, namely because:

- directors and key executives would be clearly accountable to the sole goal of maximising shareholders' wealth within what is legally permissible;
- society's welfare would be maximised when a company increases its profits, assuming that market failures – including asymmetries of information – should have been corrected by the state.

The most famous formulation of the logic summarised in the paragraph above was Milton Friedman's argument that "there is one and only one social responsibility of business – to use its resources and engage in activities designed to increase its profits so long as it stays within the rules of the game, which is to say, engages in open and free competition without deception or fraud" (Friedman, 1970[28]).

Nevertheless, at least since the Principles were first adopted in 1999, consideration of stakeholders' interests has been featured as a relevant consideration, notably in relation to the recommendations contained in Chapter 4 of the Principles on the role of stakeholders in corporate governance. Moreover, the shift of general discourse in favour of broader consideration of non-financial goals has been accelerating in recent years. In 2019, the Business Roundtable released a statement where 181 CEOs of large US corporations declared they "shared a fundamental commitment to all [their] stakeholders", including to the delivery of value to their customers, to investing in their employees, to dealing fairly with their suppliers, to supporting communities in which they work and to generating long-term value to shareholders (Business Roundtable, 2019[29]). In his 2020 annual letter, the CEO of BlackRock – the biggest asset management firm worldwide with over USD 9 trillion of assets under management – wrote to CEOs of its investee companies on corporate risks related to climate change and concluded that "companies must be deliberate and committed to embracing purpose and serving all stakeholders – your shareholders, customers, employees and the communities where you operate" (Fink, 2020[30]).

Clearly, a company's commitment to all its stakeholders is not irreconcilable with its long-term profitability. After all, loyal customers, productive employees and supportive communities are essential for a company's long-term capacity to create wealth for its shareholders. In any case, it should be noted that corporate law does not typically adhere fully to the "shareholder primacy" view, allowing companies to alternatively serve some stakeholders' interests potentially at the expense of short or long-term profitability.

In Australia, Section 181 of the Corporations Act provides that directors must exercise their powers "in good faith in the best interest of the corporation" without equating the best interests of the company with those of its shareholders. In Sweden, while Chapter 3 of the Companies Act provides that a company's "purpose is to generate a profit to be distributed among its shareholders", the Act also allows companies to establish other purposes in their articles of association" (Skog, 2015, p. 565[31]). In France, legislation amended in 2019 goes further, establishing that "the corporation must be managed in the interest of the corporation itself, while considering the social and environmental stakes of its activity" (art. 1 833, Civil Code). In the United Kingdom, Section 172 of the Companies Act provides that "a director of a company must [...] promote the success of the company for the benefit of its members as a whole, and in doing so have regard (amongst other matters) to [...] the long-term, the interests of the company's employees, [...] suppliers, customers, [...], the impact of the company's operations on the community and the environment [...]".

In Canada, the Supreme Court decided in 2008 that when considering what is in the best interests of a corporation, "directors may look to the interest of, inter alia, shareholders, employees, creditors, consumers, governments and the environment to inform their decisions" (BCE Inc. v. 1976 Debentureholders). In 2018, Section 122 of Canada's Business Corporations Act was amended to codify mentioned jurisprudence with the following language: "when acting with a view to the best interests of the corporation [...], the directors and officers of the corporation may consider, but are not limited to, the following factors: (a) the interests of shareholders, employees, retirees and pensioners, creditors, consumers, and governments; (b) the environment; and (c) the long-term interests of the corporation".

In the US state of Delaware, jurisprudence ranges from an identified director's duty to maximise shareholder profits (especially in some takeover cases, such as *Revlon* v. *MacAndrews & Forbes Holdings, Inc.*) to rulings that suggest that insufficient attention to stakeholders interests may be legally actionable (e.g. *Marchand* v. *Barnhill*). Likewise, in the *Hobby Lobby* case, the US Supreme Court explained that "while it is certainly true that a central objective of for-profit corporations is to make money, modern corporate law does not require for-profit corporations to pursue profit at the expense of everything else, and many do not do so" (Fisch and Davidoff Solomon, 2021[32]).

In any case, from a pragmatic perspective, even if an executive had a strictly defined "shareholder primacy" mandate, the business judgement rule principle[20] adopted in many legal systems and statutes authorising companies to donate money would afford the corporate executive significant discretion to consider different stakeholders' interests (Fisch and Davidoff Solomon, 2021[32]). Except for cases of conflicts of interest, it has been unlikely in practice that an executive would be held liable in court if he or she prioritised within reasonable limits a stakeholder interest at the expense of a company's current profits. The judge would typically defer to the executive's assessment of what would be likely best for the long-term profitability of the corporation.

## 1.7. Shareholders' and stakeholders' powers

With respect to a corporation's objective and its responsiveness to climate change, shareholders and stakeholders commonly have three fora where they may influence or compel managers to incorporate climate change risks into their business decision-making processes: in direct dialogue with directors and key executives, in a shareholders' meeting, and in courts.

Direct dialogue between stakeholders and management can take many forms. For instance, employees may express their views to management through elected representatives and consumers might boycott a company's products if harmful environmental practices are exposed. These initiatives could either occur spontaneously (e.g. uncoordinated interactions in social media) or supported by workers unions and civil society groups. In the case of shareholders, the initial engagement would typically take place in private meetings and correspondence, but it could escalate to public letters, proxy contests, complaints to a securities regulator and lawsuits. An individual shareholder may engage independently with a company's management (e.g. Norges Bank Investment Management follows a structured engagement process with a particular focus on climate change, water management and children's rights[21]) or a shareholder may choose to co-ordinate efforts with others (e.g. Climate Action 100+ mentioned in endnote 4 has regionally focused working groups).

Despite these differences in their engagement methods, climate change is currently a great concern both to stakeholders and investors. A 2021 survey found that 80% of people in 17 advanced economies in the Asia-Pacific, Europe and North America are willing to make at least some changes in how they live and work to help reduce the effects of climate change (Pew Research Center, 2021, p. 3[33]). As seen in Figure 1.3, climate change was the most relevant issue to prompt asset managers to seek engagement with companies in 2020. Better climate-related corporate disclosure could, therefore, be of interest to a great number of stakeholders in their engagement with companies.

In shareholders' meetings, shareholders may typically propose a resolution requiring a change in corporate policy, change the composition of the board or even alter a company's articles of association.

By mid-February 2021, shareholders had filed 66 resolutions specifically concerned with climate change for the year's US proxy season (in addition to 13 proposals about climate-related lobbying). Twenty-five of those climate-related proposals asked for the adoption of GHG emissions reduction targets in line with the Paris Agreement or, in a more indirect way, requested management to inform "if and how" the company plans to reduce emissions in line with the Agreement. In four proposals, investors asked for the establishment of annual advisory votes by shareholders on whether they approve or disapprove a company's publicly available policies and strategies with respect to climate change – in one of those proposals, this "say on climate change" would be required by the company's articles of association (As You Sow, 2021[34]).

While some of the abovementioned proposals were withdrawn (in some cases, because management took action before the annual shareholders meeting), others went to a vote and were eventually approved by a majority. For instance, 98% of votes were in favour of General Electric reporting on "if and how" it plans to achieve net zero Scope 3 GHG emissions in its supply chain by 2050, 58% in favour of Conoco Phillips adopting GHG emission goals (Scopes 1, 2 and 3[22]) and 61% in favour of Chevron substantially reducing Scope 3 GHG emissions (As You Sow, 2021[35]). At Phillips 66, a proposal requesting the company to issue a report on whether its lobbying activities are consistent with the goals of the Paris Agreement was also approved by a majority of votes (Ceres, 2021[36]). In a proxy campaign followed worldwide in June 2021, a small activist investor was able to find the necessary support from major institutional investors for the nomination of three directors to Exxon Mobil's board with the main goal of moving the company's strategy towards a lower carbon footprint (NY Times, 2021[37]).

Shareholders' proposals are often focused on specific issues and they demand relatively short-term action from management such as developing a report or a strategy, however shareholders may also propose amendments to a company's articles of association with broader and longer-term consequences. Applicable company law will evidently affect shareholders' alternatives and needs, but, for instance, articles of association may require a long-term view from management or even explicitly allow executives' consideration of non-shareholder interests irrespective of their effect on shareholders' wealth. For example, Switzerland-based Nestlé's articles of association provide the company "shall, in pursuing its business purpose, aim for long-term, sustainable value creation" (article two, item 3).

Meaningfully diverting a company from a profit-making goal would, however, create a number of challenges, some of which are further covered in this report. That is why some jurisdictions have amended their legislation with the aim to offer a legal structure fit for for-profit corporations willing to adopt objectives other than simply maximising long-term profits, while allowing shareholders to retain the same degree of control of corporate decision-making, such as electing directors and amending the articles of association. This is the case of public benefit corporations (PBC) in Delaware and *sociétés à mission* in France.

In Delaware, for-profit corporations may, since 2013, be incorporated as or be converted into PBCs, which represents a legal obligation to "be managed in a manner that balances the stockholders' pecuniary interests, the best interests of those materially affected by the corporation's conduct, and the public benefit or public benefits identified in its [articles of association]" (Delaware General Corporation Law, Chapter 1, subchapter XV). In addition to identifying one or more public benefits to be promoted by the corporation in its articles of association, PBCs also have the two following obligations: (i) in any stock certificate and in every notice of a shareholders meeting, they must clearly note they are a PBC; (ii) the board of directors should at least every two years report to shareholders on the promotion of the public benefits identified in the articles of association (these articles may also demand a third-party verification of the public interests' fulfilment). Any action to enforce directors' and key executives' obligation to balance pecuniary, stakeholders' and public interests may only be brought by plaintiffs owning 2% of the PBC's outstanding shares (limited to USD 2 million in shares if the corporation is listed).

In 2020, Delaware statutory rules were amended in order to facilitate the conversion of conventional corporations into PBCs (Littenberg et al., 2020[38]). Nowadays, an existing conventional corporation needs the approval of only a majority of votes in a shareholders meeting (unless the articles of association provide otherwise) to convert, merge or consolidate with or into a PBC (the same threshold applies for a PBC becoming a conventional corporation). Originally, the threshold established by Delaware law was of 90% of the outstanding shares. Likewise, shareholders who opposed or did not vote for the conversion of a conventional corporation to a PBC no longer have a specific statutory appraisal right (i.e. the right to sell their shares back to the corporation at a fair price).

As of September 2021, 207 private PBCs incorporated in Delaware contained the words "public benefit corporation" or "PBC" in their business names.[23] While the number of listed PBCs incorporated in Delaware is so far limited to seven[24] (with market capitalisation ranging from approximately USD 700 million to USD 50 billion as of September 2021), it may be too soon to assess the impact of the recent changes to Delaware statutory rules to facilitate such conversions. Veeva Systems, a tech company which is the most valuable listed PBC incorporated in Delaware with USD 47.5 billion market value, states in its articles of association that the "specific public benefits to be promoted by the Corporation are to provide products and services that are intended to help make the industries we serve more productive, and to create high-quality employment opportunities in the communities in which we operate".

In France, for-profit corporations may, since 2019, adopt social and environmental objectives in their articles of association and, therefore, register with the business name of *société à mission* (art. L.210, Commercial Code). There are three main conditions for a corporation to be registered with this name: (i) inclusion of social and environmental objectives into the articles of association; (ii) establishment of a committee – with the participation of at least one employee – responsible exclusively for verifying and reporting to the annual shareholders meeting whether the company fulfils its non-financial goals; (iii) verification by an accredited independent third-party of whether the company fulfilled its non-financial goals and report to the annual shareholders meeting. If a corporation does not comply with any of those requirements or the independent third-party concludes a non-financial goal was not fulfilled, public prosecutors or any interested party – which could arguably include stakeholders – may request the suppression of *société à mission* from the corporation's business name.

As of the second quarter of 2021, there were 206 *sociétés à mission* of which just three are listed companies. A majority of *sociétés à mission* is private and employ less than 50 employees[25]

(L'Observatoire des Sociétés à Mission, 2021[39]). Among one of the early adopters of the *société à mission* designation, Danone amended its articles of association in June 2020 and included, among its social and environmental goals, to contribute "to the fight against climate change" and to develop "everyday products accessible to as many people as possible" (art. one, item III).

In some cases, stakeholders may decide a lawsuit is the best or only solution to a disagreement with a company's management. It may be either because a company's management was irresponsive to a legitimate request or due to the fact compensation for an irreversible damage is warranted. As a general rule, only shareholders have standing to sue with respect to the violation of directors' fiduciary duties, but stakeholders may have a number of other grounds to bring a suit against a corporation or its managers (some examples below).

Corporations were defendants in 18 climate change-related court cases filed globally between May 2020 and May 2021 (14 in the United States and 4 in other countries).[26] Climate-related corporate litigation has been traditionally focused on major carbon-emitters (there are 33 ongoing cases worldwide against the largest fossil fuel companies), and applicants have most commonly argued defendants were liable for past contributions to climate change (for instance, municipalities in the United States requesting damages to pay for climate change adaptation). An increasing number of claims, however, have also covered the current fulfilment of fiduciary duties and due diligence obligations by companies and their managers in industries other than oil and gas, and cement (notably pension funds, banks and asset managers as defendants), including claims of insufficient disclosure of climate-related information, inconsistencies between discourse and action on climate change, and inadequate management of climate risks (Setzer J and Higham C, 2021[40]).

As an example of recent litigation strategies focused on the fulfilment of fiduciary and care duties, a member of an Australian pension fund claimed the fund was not disclosing and managing climate change risks as it would have been required according to broadly defined duties of care and transparency under company and superannuation industry laws. In a settlement in 2020, the fund agreed to report on climate in line with TCFD recommendations and to adopt a net zero 2050 goal (*McVeigh* v. *REST*). In another example, in 2021, the District Court of the Hague, answering to a suit brought by seven environmental NGOs and more than 17 000 citizens, ordered an oil and gas company based in the Netherlands to reduce its own emissions and its customers' emissions in accordance with the goals of the Paris Agreement as an obligation derived from the standard of care laid down in the Dutch Civil Code (*Milieudefensie* et al. v. *Royal Dutch Shell*) (LSE, 2020[41]). In establishing the duty of care for the concrete case, the court explicitly referenced the OECD Guidelines for Multinational Enterprises, quoting the opening recommendation in the Environment chapter on taking "due account of the need to protect the environment" (OECD, 2011[42]).

# 2 Key issues

This chapter contextualises the climate transition within the debate on corporate short-termism. It also presents how existing financial standards already require disclosure of climate change's impact on a company's business, and discusses the main drawbacks in existing transparency regimes. The chapter summarises the main concepts of materiality for corporate disclosure and discusses the main challenges related to the adoption of each concept. It then investigates the existing difficulties due the lack of comparability of companies' sustainability disclosure and assesses new developments in sustainability standard-setting. It proposes four models to understand how director fiduciary duties are defined in different jurisdictions, and investigates their positive aspects and disadvantages. The chapter then focuses on how shareholders may exercise their rights on climate-related matters. Finally it highlights how green bonds, voluntary carbon credit markets and well-developed capital markets may help in financing the climate transition.

## 2.1. Short-termism

A heated public debate has taken place during the last decade on whether public companies' senior executives and shareholders are excessively focused on short-term results to the detriment of investment in long-term projects (so-called "short-termism"). Some have argued that short-termism is not a problem with economy-damaging consequences, as demonstrated by the recent success of innovative companies in public equity markets (Bebchuk, 2021[43]) and steadily rising investments in R&D (Roe, 2018[44]). Others, however, disagree with this assessment, and suggest, for instance, that there is a misalignment between executive pay and long-term results that has led to corporations investing less in projects with long-term payoffs such as building new factories (Strine Jr., 2017[45]).

Evidence shows that investment as a share of GDP by non-financial companies has been sluggish, growing only slightly since 2005, while R&D has significantly increased during the same period (OECD, 2021, p. 32[46]). Other studies also find evidence of underinvestment both in the Euro Area when measuring net investment as a share of GDP (Kalemli-Ozcan, Laeven and Moreno, 2019[47]) and in the United States when comparing investment to corporate valuations and profitability (Gutiérrez and Philippon, 2016[48]). Finally, studies have found that in the US private companies invest less than public companies, particularly in R&D (Feldman et al., 2018[49]).

While contributing to the policy debate on short-termism is beyond the scope of this report, it is important to discuss how climate change and short-termism[27] (if indeed an economy-wide concern) may be related.

To begin with a more pessimistic perspective, better disclosure on climate-related risks and broad legal provisions for management to consider the environment may not achieve much if the incentives for directors, senior executives and investors are to act only on what is relevant for short-term financial results. In the same way financial reports' information on R&D expenditure and capital investment may not be enough to incentivise a long-term view of senior executives and shareholders, it could be argued that data on GHG corporate emissions would not be sufficient to improve corporations' climate-related policies. According to this line of argument, corporations might eventually move towards a lower carbon footprint but most likely only if and when public policy or stakeholders' preferences have a meaningful short-term impact on a company's balance sheet.

In some circumstances, better disclosure of climate-related risks and changes in company law (or at least how the legislation is interpreted) might indeed be effective regardless of executives' and shareholders' time horizons. For instance, transparency could lead environmentally conscious employees or consumers to steer away from an above-average polluting company, potentially reducing, respectively, its productivity and revenues and, therefore, giving a competitive edge to greener companies. Likewise, better information on corporate climate-related risks might make policy makers act sooner rather than later after realising the concrete physical risks companies face. Lastly, some individual court rulings involving major carbon-emitters may actually have a meaningful impact (e.g. the District Court of the Hague's decision mentioned in Section 1.7).

In addition, such disclosure may impact the investment and voting decisions of asset owners and investors, who seem to be concerned with sustainability and climate-related risks when managing their portfolios (see Table 1.1 and Figure 1.3). This might be the case either because many shareholders actually have a long-term view, or due to the fact that climate change has become a short-term concern for corporations' financial results (or a combination of both factors). What remains to be seen – within the short-termism debate – is whether and how quickly investors' concerns about climate change will translate into changes in directors' and key executives' decision-making processes. While it is still an open question, there is evidence that shareholders are making themselves heard rather quickly, including through changes in executive compensation plans (as seen in Table 1.7, over a quarter of the largest listed companies globally already use ESG measures in their plans) and shareholders' proposals for companies to adopt GHG emissions targets (see Section 1.7).

## 2.2. Mainstream transparency regimes

Financial standards already require disclosure on how climate change may impact a company's business in some circumstances. A US Financial Accounting Standards Board staff paper states that "an entity may consider the effects of certain material ESG matters, similar to how an entity considers other changes in its business and operating environment that have a material direct or indirect effect on the financial statements and notes thereto" (FASB, 2021, p. 3[50]). For instance, companies will have to consider whether reduced demand for products with high carbon footprints might impact the fair valuation of their assets, and banks may need to reassess expected credit losses for loans to companies in carbon-intensive sectors if a new environmental policy is expected to affect them. As an example, UK-based BP recognised an impairment loss of almost USD 13 billion in 2020 primarily relating to losses incurred with respect to changes in expected cash-flows of production and development assets due to lower oil and gas price and production assumptions in the context of a transition to a lower carbon economy (BP, 2020, pp. 166, 179[51]).

What may be less evident is that companies might need to disclose in the notes to their financial statements more than relevant changes in their balance sheets whenever the information is material for investors, including assumptions with respect to the future. As clarified by an IASB board member, for example, "a company may need to explain its judgement that it was not necessary to factor climate change into the impairment assumptions, or how estimates of expected future cash flows, risk adjustments to discount rates or useful lives have, or have not, been affected by climate change" (Anderson, 2019, p. 9[52]). Echoing this reasoning, an International Auditing and Assurance Standards Board (IAASB) staff alert highlights that "[i]f information, such as climate change, can affect user decision-making, then this information should be deemed as 'material' and warrant disclosure in the financial statements, regardless of their numerical impact" (IAASB, 2020, p. 3[53]).

As a general rule, financial reporting standards do not require a structured disclosure on strategy, risk management and non-financial information (e.g. GHG emissions) that may be relevant for investors to assess a company's business perspectives and risks. Moreover, management often has limited ability to communicate perspectives for the future in the management commentary to the financial reports and in other regulatory filings. Those features of the current transparency regimes have their justifications, but it is important to consider their drawbacks and observe how they relate to the climate change corporate disclosure debate.

In some circumstances, limiting the ability of managers to communicate their perspectives for the future is a sensible policy. After all, senior executives have strong incentives to convince investors that their recent results were positive and that the future is even brighter: their remuneration and security in their positions depend on that. In relation to past results, there might be some controversy (e.g. if an increase in profits can be attributed to management's efforts) but, overall, books of accounts provide a relatively sound basis for assessing previous results. Nevertheless, the future is even more uncertain. It is often a mere educated guess whether a new product or factory will prove to be profitable.

A backward-looking transparency regime, however, has its weaknesses with respect to reducing the informational asymmetry between management and investors. While the future is evidently uncertain for managers, they have probably invested resources designing strategies and analysing risks, and their conclusions might be valuable for investors. This is especially relevant for risks that do not frequently occur (so-called "tail risks") because they will seldom materialise in financial statements but, when they do, they might have a significant impact on a company's businesses. Those "tail risks" might be financial ones (e.g. a sudden major move in interest rates), risks related to a company's core businesses (e.g. flooding in a major factory), and environmental and social risks.

A number of capital markets regulators have considered the importance of management communicating on material risks faced by public companies, but existing disclosure has been sometimes insufficient for two main reasons: (i) rules demanding disclosure of material risks (e.g. in annual forms and initial public offerings (IPO) prospectuses) do not typically specify which types of risks and how they should be presented to investors; (ii) enforcement of those disclosure rules may have incentivised an opaque disclosure.

Not being prescriptive on which risks to disclose and how to present them to investors has a clear benefit. Different economic sectors face different types of risks and, in some circumstances, even companies in the same economic sector might encounter distinct perils, which may require flexibility to properly assess risks and disclose them. Nevertheless, managers may have the incentive to downplay existing risks because a riskier company has a higher cost of capital and, therefore, smaller market value.

The remedy to the problem above has been to rely on enforcement – by public regulators and through the courts – to discourage directors and key executives from misrepresenting the material risks of the companies they serve. For example, if a company did not include in the prospectus of its IPO the risk of flooding where it has its major factory, shareholders might file a lawsuit demanding compensation if there is indeed a disruption in production due to a major flooding. Shareholders will have to prove that mentioned risk was material for the company at the moment of the IPO, but what is material in a concrete case may be interpreted in different ways in the absence of a clear framework.

In order to avoid referred litigation risks, senior executives may conclude that it is in their interest to refer to many types of risks (regardless of whether material or not) but, at the same time, use boilerplate language that would not allow investors to effectively assess a company's "tail risks" or competitors to identify a company's strategic weakness. If demanded by regulators or the judiciary, managers would be able to point to a company's public document where the materialised risk was referred to. However, because the material risks were not well detailed, investors would find it difficult to apply adequate discounts to a company's value because of existing "tail risks". Of course, a low quality disclosure of risks may actually mean that investors will apply a meaningful discount in their valuation of a company simply because they do not have access to sufficient information, which would be detrimental to the development of the capital market.

A number of regulators have rules to improve the clarity in listed companies' filings, such as the US SEC in its note to rule §230.421 stating that "vague 'boilerplate' explanations that are imprecise and readily subject to different interpretations" should be avoided in prospectuses. Likewise, as one of its main messages, an OECD report on corporate governance and the global financial crisis concluded that "the overall results of risk assessments should be appropriately disclosed in a transparent and understandable fashion [and] disclosure of risk factors should identify those most relevant to the company's strategy" (2010, p. 15[54]). While regulators' efforts are welcomed, there is not any instant and permanent solution to the problem. For instance, an analysis of 2 751 IPOs of operating companies between 1996 and 2015 in the United States found that there was an average 32% – with 41% at the 75th percentile – of text similarity in the "risk factors" section of a prospectus compared to all prospectuses of companies in the same industry in the preceding year (McClane, 2019, pp. 229, 277[55]).

To some extent, the current regulatory movement and investors' demand for better disclosure of climate-related risks might be seen as a way to compensate for a transparency regime that has not been completely successful in informing the market on many future risks including climate-related ones. In that sense, forward-looking information requirements may be important considerations when (and if) a jurisdiction decides to enact a disclosure rule for climate-related information.

## 2.3. Materiality

An essential part of any reporting system is the criteria to choose which pieces of information must be communicated to end-users. In the case of companies, the term often used to refer to this assessment is "materiality": whether a piece of information is material enough for its primary users to justify the costs of collecting the information and disclosing it. Clearly, a case-by-case costs and benefits analysis of the materiality of every piece of information would not be feasible, so the implementation of the materiality concept depends to a large extent on reporting standards, securities regulators' guidance and practices widely accepted in the capital markets.

Information has traditionally been considered material if it could reasonably be expected to influence an investor's or a creditor's analysis of a company's future cash flows. For instance, IASB provides that "information is material if omitting, misstating or obscuring it could reasonably be expected to influence the decisions that the primary users of general purpose financial reports make on the basis of those reports, which provide financial information about a specific reporting entity" (2018, p. A22[14]). In an often-cited precedent, the US Supreme Court clarified that "an omitted fact is material if there is a substantial likelihood that a reasonable shareholder would consider it important in deciding how to vote. [...] Put another way, there must be a substantial likelihood that the disclosure of the omitted fact would have been viewed by the reasonable investor as having significantly altered the 'total mix' of information made available" (*TSC Industries, Inc.* v. *Northway, Inc.*). This materiality concept can be labelled "financial materiality", and, as detailed in Table 1.3, not only financial reporting standards but also a number of ESG reporting frameworks and standards adopt a "financial materiality" approach.

More recently, a "double materiality" concept has been adopted in some sustainability reporting frameworks, defining as material information that – in addition to being financially relevant to investors – would be pertinent to multiple stakeholders' understanding of a company's effect on the environment and on people (e.g. for consumers, employees and communities). For example, the 2014 EU Non-Financial Reporting Directive provides that a company subject to the directive is required to disclose information "to the extent necessary for an understanding of the undertaking's development, performance, position and impact of its activity, relating to, as a minimum, environmental, social and employee matters, respect for human rights, anti-corruption and bribery matters" (Article 19a, item 1).

The G20/OECD Principles of Corporate Governance offer two alternative definitions of materiality in the annotations to Principle V. One closer to "financial materiality", suggesting that "material information can [...] be defined as information that a reasonable *investor* would consider important in making an *investment or voting decision*" (emphasis added). The alternative definition is more open and, while not necessarily adhering to a "double materiality" perspective, potentially includes stakeholders as main recipients of corporate information: "material information can be defined as information whose omission or misstatement could influence the *economic decisions* taken by *users of information*" (emphasis added). Likewise, with respect to the disclosure of sustainability information, annotations to Principle V.A.2 say that "companies are *encouraged* to disclose policies and performance relating to business ethics, the environment and, where material to the company, social issues, human rights and other public policy commitments" (emphasis added).

OECD Responsible Business Conduct (RBC) instruments also reflect public reporting expectations in the context of due diligence processes. The MNE Guidelines include expectations that enterprises publicly report information on all material matters regarding their activities, structure, financial situation, performance, ownership and governance, as well as additional information on their social and environmental policies and their performance in relation to these. OECD due diligence guidance clarifies the expectation to publicly disclose due diligence policies, processes, and activities conducted to identify and address actual or potential adverse impacts, including the findings and outcomes of those activities (OECD, 2018[56]).

While in theory clearly distinct, the frontiers between financial and double materiality may be rather fluid in practice. For instance, in what constitutes one aspect of "dynamic materiality" (WEF, 2020, p. 8[57]), a risk that does not seem to be financially material in a moment in time (e.g. GHG emissions in a country with a poor environmental track-record) may gradually or quickly become financially relevant if the social context changes (in the same example, if a climate-conscious political leadership comes to power). In some contexts, economically irrelevant ESG risks that are material for a society may be expected at some point to become financially material for a company, either through society's pressure for a switch in public policy (e.g. regulation that makes companies internalise externalities) or consumers' and employees' change of preferences (making companies voluntarily change their businesses). To some extent, therefore, the time horizon used in the materiality analysis seems to be also key: the longer the time horizon, the larger the potential for overlap between financial and double materiality (IOSCO, 2021, pp. 28-30[58]).

Regardless of the time horizon, it should also be noted that even in the shorter term there might also be a significant overlap between information items that are material both to a company's cash flows and to society as a whole. To take the example of a company in the energy sector, Canada-based Suncor disclosed in 2021 its Scope 1 GHG emissions and energy consumption as required both by SASB and GRI standards (respectively, as seen in Table 1.3, they follow a financial and double materiality concepts). The same company also disclosed, among climate-related items, Scopes 2 and 3 GHG emissions and the energy intensity of its operations, but, in those cases, only to align itself with the GRI Standards (Suncor Energy, 2021, pp. 76-87[59]).

By definition, "double materiality" requires wider disclosure than "financial materiality" because the former includes the latter (the example in the paragraph above concretely shows it). Since collecting information and disclosing it present a relatively fixed cost for a company (somewhat independent from its size), a mandatory requirement to disclose ESG information according to a double materiality standard would represent a greater relative cost for SMEs when compared to larger companies. Moreover, if disclosure is only mandatory for listed companies, it might represent a disincentive for companies to go public.

Another challenge for policy makers considering to mandate an ESG disclosure regime based on "double materiality" rather than "financial materiality" would be the transition and longer-term costs it would create for some key capital markets actors other than companies, namely for securities regulators and auditors. First, there would be a short-term cost for changing systems and rules that were typically based on the assumption that corporate information to be disclosed should be material for investors. For instance, securities regulators that have a legal mandate only to protect investors and to maintain fair, efficient and transparent markets might need to have their powers enlarged to also include addressing systemic risks (climate change can arguably be considered a systemic risk as discussed in Section 1.3) or non-financially material ESG risks more broadly. Also as an example, audit firms and professional accountancy organisations would probably need to establish systems to assess the materiality of each different ESG risk, since there would not be anymore the financial impact as the "unit of account" for all risks and opportunities.

Second, if key capital market actors become responsible for analysing information beyond their core expertise in corporate finance, they might become less efficient as a result. For example, securities regulators would need to supervise risks that have been (and will probably continue to be) overseen by environmental agencies, potentially duplicating work and offering conflicting guidance on non-financial materiality in some circumstances. Likewise, the assessment of what is material for society as a whole requires the use of techniques, reference points and data from the public policy discipline, which are not often mastered by corporate finance experts and may be expensive (e.g. surveys to assess the preferences of a great number of individuals).

Much of the relevance of the discussion above would dissipate if investors were as concerned with their investees' impact on society as they are with their long-term financial results. If this were the case, a company's impact on society and the environment would necessarily become financially material because investors would be willing to accept smaller returns in exchange for positive contributions for society (i.e. a company's cost of capital would be smaller). However, evidence so far is that investors continue to be by and large more concerned with the financial performance of their assets (as seen in Table 1.2, strategies that often accept a tangible trade-off between wealth creation and better ESG results do not currently represent a significant share of assets under management) and investors are especially interested in sustainability information that is financially material (as shown in Figure 1.5, TCFD recommendations and SASB Standards – which follow a financial materiality criterion – are by far the preferred ESG framework by institutional investors). This is also corroborated by a recent survey of 325 institutional asset managers and asset owners globally where only 34% of them agreed to be "willing to accept a lower rate of return in exchange for societal or environmental benefit" (49% disagreed with the sentence, while 17% were neutral) (Chalmers, Cox and Picard, 2021, p. 4[60]).

Some policy makers have suggested that there may be some space for a compromise between either adopting the financial materiality approach or the double materiality concept. A definition of materiality could rely *not solely* on the expected impact of a piece of information on how investors assess the cash-flows of a company and their volatility, but also encompass the most relevant considerations an investor makes when trading securities and voting in a shareholder meeting. The financial results of a for-profit company are generally a major consideration for investors, but a limited number of other considerations could also be commonly relevant to many investors (and therefore considered material for a company). Adopting such a flexible definition of materiality may be practical and would allow companies to adapt the content of their sustainability disclosure over time in line with changes in shareholder preferences.

Considering the concerns about how interested and effective investors may be addressing businesses' impacts on climate that are not financially material, many stakeholders and some policy makers continue to seek additional sustainability disclosure beyond that which is material. However, it should be noted that the continued adoption of a financial materiality criterion for the disclosure regime of listed companies does not preclude environmental agencies and other self-regulatory or public bodies from enacting transparency standards guided by the interests of society as a whole. There would be three reasons in favour of governments keeping the traditional division of labour between capital market regulators focused on investor interests and environmental agencies protecting society concerns. First, this division would avoid the transition and long-term costs inherent in the adoption of an ESG disclosure regime based on "double materiality" as mentioned above. Second, since companies' externalities are relevant for society regardless of whether corporations are listed, a disclosure requirement applicable both for listed and privately held companies may be more effective and level the playing field. Third, government agencies with the experience in protecting consumers and employees may be more effective in communicating with them. For instance, easy-to-read information about a refrigerator's energy consumption in a store is arguably more useful for an environmentally conscious consumer than the disclosure of Scope 3 GHG emissions in a sustainability report from the company that manufactured it.

## 2.4. ESG accounting and reporting frameworks

As covered in detail in Chapter 3, many jurisdictions do not currently mandate the use of a specific ESG or climate-related risks reporting framework or standard. This freedom has led corporations to adopt a number of different standards or, in some cases, disclose only some information items foreseen in a specific standard (see often used standards by large US companies in Figure 1.4). Moreover, 9% of 1 400 large listed companies globally did not report any level of sustainability information in 2019 (see Section 1.4 for more information).

The lack of comparability between companies' sustainability information harms investors' capacity to adequately value each company and, therefore, to decide how to allocate their capital and engage with companies. In other words, capital markets are less efficient if companies do not disclose sustainability information that is financially material or if their disclosures are difficult to compare. Likewise, disclosure of material risks is essential for investors to effectively manage the aggregate risks of their portfolios, and for financial stability supervisors to anticipate systemic risks (see Section 1.3 on NGFS' recommendation for regulators to achieve "robust and internationally consistent climate and environment-related disclosure").

The importance of comparability was underlined in a survey recently conducted by the International Organization of Securities Commissions (IOSCO) of 60 asset managers across 19 jurisdictions on sustainability information for investment decisions. The survey identified the creation and adoption of a mandatory common international standard reporting as the most important area for improvement with respect to sustainability (IOSCO, 2021, p. 18[58]). Similarly, a 2019 survey with investors representing 27 asset managers and 30 asset owners from Asia, Europe and the United States found that 75% of them agreed with the statement that "there should be one sustainability-reporting standard" and 82% concurred that "companies should be required by law to issue sustainability reports" (McKinsey & Co., 2019, p. 3[61]).

In a very concrete way, the adoption of multiple ESG or climate-related risks reporting standards also creates costs for corporations, which may have to either comply with different reporting standards or respond to ad hoc information requests by institutional investors interested in comparing results and business prospects of their investees. Moreover, directors and key executives may be interested in benchmarking their non-financial performance against their peers in order to better identify where improvement is needed or claim their success if their results are above-average. This may explain why, in the same aforementioned 2019 survey, 58% of executives representing 50 companies from Asia, Europe and the United States agreed with the statement that "there should be one sustainability-reporting standard" and 66% concurred that "companies should be required by law to issue sustainability reports" (McKinsey & Co., 2019, p. 3[61]).

As detailed in the Chapter 3, some jurisdictions have already established regulations or initiated public consultations or legislative proposals to mandate companies to disclose sustainability information according to a specific reporting standard. There are two main challenges in such processes: (i) the definition of the group of companies that will be subject to the new disclosure obligation; (ii) the co-ordination across jurisdictions to adopt – if not the same reporting standard – at least to develop some core guidance and metrics that could be identical in all markets.

As discussed above, disclosure requirements often represent a greater relative cost for SMEs when compared to larger companies and, if disclosure is only mandatory for listed companies, sustainability disclosure requirements might represent a disincentive for some companies to go public. With respect to disclosure costs, it should be noted that there are not only direct costs such as developing internal control systems and hiring an external auditor, but there are also indirect costs such as revealing information that may be useful for competitors. Having those challenges in mind, policy makers have devised financial information rules that are flexible according to the size of the company or its stage of development, for instance providing a waiver from some non-essential disclosure requirements for emerging growth companies (OECD, 2018, pp. 17-18[62]).

In considering a path towards greater comparability, the experience of adopting IFRS Standards across most jurisdictions on a global basis can serve as a reference. In total, 144 jurisdictions required the use of IFRS Standards for all or most domestic listed companies as of 2018 (IFRS Foundation, 2018[63]). This successful experience is probably the reason why the IFRS Foundation November 2021 announcement that it would amend its constitution to accommodate an International Sustainability Standards Board (ISSB) within its structure has been met with enthusiasm by a number of jurisdictions and the IOSCO (see more below).

The ISSB will build on the work of existing investor-focused sustainability reporting initiatives to set IFRS Sustainability Disclosure Standards. The IFRS Foundation's recently amended constitution provides that IFRS Sustainability Disclosure Standards "are intended to result in the provision of high-quality, transparent and comparable information [...] in sustainability disclosures that is useful to investors and other participants in the world's capital markets in making economic decisions" (item 2.a). Likewise, by June 2022 this new board will merge with the CDSB, SASB Standards Board and <IR> Framework Board to consolidate their technical expertise, content, staff and other resources (for more information on those boards, see Table 1.3). In this context, the Technical Readiness Working Group (TRWG) – a group formed by the IFRS Foundation Trustees to undertake preparatory work for the ISSB[28] – has already published a prototype climate standard building on the TCFD recommendations and another prototype document on general disclosure requirements for consideration by the ISSB in its initial work plan (IFRS Foundation, 2021[64]).

Of special interest is the IFRS Foundation's views of a "building blocks" approach and an initial priority for climate-related matters in the work of the planned ISSB (IFRS Foundation, 2021, p. 5[65]). This would mean that ISSB would co-operate with standard-setters from key jurisdictions in order to have a globally consistent set of core standards that would allow the comparability of sustainability reports in those jurisdictions, and expect that standard-setters from smaller markets would eventually adhere to this global reporting baseline. The "building blocks" strategy may also allow, for instance, globally accepted standards based on a financial materiality criterion but with the flexibility for complementary regional or national standards requiring disclosure on matters deemed material only from a "double materiality" perspective.

The IFRS Foundation's decision to initially focus on climate-related matters before working towards other ESG issues is also interesting from a practical point of view. Local standard-setters may be willing to wait for the establishment of global sustainability standards by the ISSB – instead of creating their own – if they foresee in the short term a standard on one of the most pressing ESG issues. Indeed, as shown in Section 1.5 and Figure 1.6, despite some regional variations, some climate-related risks are financially material for an important share of listed companies by market value globally (more than other environmental risks), representing 65% of the total market capitalisation.

Finally, if disclosed ESG information is not assured by a third-party based on robust methodologies, it could undermine confidence in the disclosed information and the possibility to compare sustainability reports between companies. As noted in Section 1.4, only around half of large listed companies that disclosed sustainability information in 2019 provided some level of assurance by a third party. Moreover, only a small minority of these assurance engagements offered "reasonable" assurances ("reasonable" is the level expected from audits of financial reports[29]). While reasonable assurance for all disclosed sustainability information may not be achievable with the stroke of a pen, there may be space for short-term advancements with mandatory assurance for some key climate-related metrics such as GHG emissions. With clearer sustainability standards and more experience by all capital markets service providers, however, greater convergence of the level of assurance between financial and sustainability reports may be expected in the longer term.

## 2.5. Directors' fiduciary duties

While business reality is complex, corporate law and capital markets regulation generally present a simplified definition of directors' and key executives' duties in order to make them functional. Corporate laws often provide – in a language similar to the one adopted by G20/OECD Principle VI.A – that "board members should act on a fully informed basis, in good faith, with due diligence and care" ("duty of care") and "in the best interest of the company and the shareholders" ("duty of loyalty"). As a whole, these duties of care and loyalty are often referred to as directors' and executives' "fiduciary duties".

As detailed between Sections 1.6 and 1.7, company laws in different jurisdictions vary in relation to who is effectively the recipient of directors' and executives' fiduciary duty of loyalty. For ease of discussion, one could outline four models:[30]

a. At one end of the spectrum, company law and judiciary precedents may fully adhere to the "shareholder primacy" view, obliging directors to consider only shareholders' financial interests (e.g. some Delaware precedents in takeover cases) while complying with the applicable law and ethical standards. This still requires attention to non-shareholders' interests, but only to the extent that those interests may be relevant for the creation of long-term shareholder value.

b. Close to the approach above, loyalty could be largely to shareholders' financial interests but directors would have to *consider* stakeholders' interests, and the social and environmental stakes of a company's activity (e.g. the language in the French Civil Code). *Consideration* here might be interpreted as careful thought given to stakeholders' interests to a degree that is equal or higher than well-established standards (such as those in the MNE Guidelines) but still falling short of what a social planner would prefer for society as a whole.

c. A third approach would be to amplify the group of recipients of the duty of loyalty. Directors would therefore be equally devoted to shareholders and to a number of defined stakeholders, such as employees and customers. This may imply, in a concrete case, directors making a decision that would meaningfully reduce long-term shareholder value in order to benefit a group of stakeholders.

d. At the other end of the spectrum, directors would need to balance shareholders' financial interests with the best interests of stakeholders (just like in the third approach above), and, in addition, to fulfil a number of specified public interests (e.g. PBCs in Delaware and *société à mission* in France). In relation to these public interests, directors would be responsible for maximising social welfare in a manner virtually similar to what public servants do.

Zooming out from any individual legal system, there are positive aspects and drawbacks to all of these models. Model "a" above has a significant advantage: directors and key executives are clearly accountable to the sole goal of maximising shareholders' wealth within what is legally and ethically permissible. This model still leaves significant discretion to managers – because what is ethically required and expected to increase long-term value may not be evident – but there are some relatively good proxies to assess management's performance, such as equity prices and profits during a reasonable time period.

The main drawback of model "a" is that, if there are relevant market failures, the maximisation of profits by a company may reduce welfare for society as a whole or even the long-term value of its shareholders' portfolios. With respect to society's welfare, for example, if there are no adequate public policies to reduce GHG emissions, companies may emit more than what would be socially desirable – taking into account the trade-off between economic development and climate-related risks – with the goal of maximising profits. In regard to an investor's portfolio, for instance, the wealth created by a profit-maximising major carbon emitter company may be more than off-set by losses in the long-term value of other investee companies affected by climate change (e.g. a hotel chain that would need to write off assets affected by rising sea levels).

Models "b", "c" and "d" – with their own peculiarities – attempt to solve the challenge mentioned in the paragraph above. Recognising that contracts between the company and stakeholders are often incomplete, and that the state – especially in developing countries and with respect to highly complex industries – may not always be able to implement optimal or fully enforceable regulation, those three models impose a duty for corporate managers to consider or fulfil stakeholders' and society's interests. If managers have adequate incentives to consider or fulfil these interests, the solution of expanding the duty of loyalty might be advisable because directors and key executives are arguably the most well-informed individuals with respect to their company's risks, opportunities and societal impact.

When compared to model "a", however, the decision-making process of managers and the evaluation of their results may grow exponentially more complex in the other three models because non-financial results are extremely difficult to compare and value, both with other non-financial results as well as with financial results. For example, if a company faces the alternative between upgrading a factory to emit 1 Mt $CO_2$ less a year or preserve 40 000 hectares of tropical forest, it may not be evident what the best option for society would be. The $CO_2$ storage capacity of the forest could be estimated, but there would also be benefits – such as protecting biodiversity and water security with the forest preservation option – that are not straightforward to compare to $CO_2$ storage. Moreover, there would also be the option of not adopting any of the two alternatives, which may increase profits and dividends to shareholders. This could allow the shareholders themselves to donate more money to an environmental philanthropic organisation or increase tax revenues that governments may use to support environmental objectives.

The greatest risk of models "b", "c" and "d" is, therefore, threefold. First, managers would need to make decisions on projects that are not necessarily within their expertise. For instance, running a steelmaking business efficiently may have little to do with cost-effectively reforesting. While expertise can be developed internally or outsourced in some cases, at C-level positions and on the board new issues to consider will inevitably mean more time demanded from individuals who may already struggle with a great number of responsibilities. Second, while the economics discipline has found creative ways to value public goods and human life, the technical and ethical challenges of doing so are seldom trivial. For example, it may not be difficult for a manager of a European company to assess the trade-off between profits and $CO_2$ emissions, because the market for carbon permits is active in Europe, but it may be more challenging in other parts of the world. Third, if shareholders and stakeholders cannot properly compare financial and non-financial results, directors and key executives may become less accountable. In the same example, a CEO in a steel-making business may argue that below-average return on equity was due to a stellar environmental performance and not to their incompetency in leading the company.

While the risks summarised in the paragraph above may be to some extent manageable, this could still be costly and present at least one unintended consequence. With respect to costs, for instance, in order to increase managers' accountability, companies may be required by legislators to hire an independent third-party to regularly verify whether management fulfilled their non-financial goals. The unintended consequences are difficult to assess because the number and size of companies with legally actionable non-financial goals – as seen in Section 1.7 – is still small, but one could conceive the role courts may have in enforcing a broadened duty of loyalty such as in models "c" and "d".

How common court cases involving managers' duty to fulfil non-financial goals may be depends on many factors (e.g. if only shareholders or others have a standing to sue, the standard of review adopted by the courts,[31] and the extent to which a jurisdiction's legal framework is conducive to the use of private enforcement), but the fact is that judges may eventually need to decide whether managers have abided by their broadened duty of loyalty. This control by the courts, however, might face limitations for the same reasons that may have justified – as argued above – broadening the fiduciary duties in the first place. If the executive and the legislative branches of government – with all their multidisciplinary experts and public consultations – were unable to enact optimal regulation to reduce market failures, it is an open question whether professionals with legal training could do better when assessing corporate executives' decisions. Moreover, as previously mentioned, evaluating trade-offs between non-financial goals may be technically or ethically challenging (e.g. closing a coal-fired power station that is the only source of employment in a poor community in order to fight climate change), and it is not clear-cut whether the courts (or, in the first place, directors and key executives) would have the social legitimacy to be the arbiter in those cases.

Finally, it should be noted that – as well explored in the G20/OECD Principles – directors are responsible for overseeing the company's risk management, which involves "oversight of the accountabilities and responsibilities for managing risks, specifying the types and degree of risk that a company is willing to accept in pursuit of its goals, and how it will manage the risks it creates through its operations and relationships" (annotation to Principle VI.D.1). Evidently, therefore, if climate-change risks are financially material for a company, they would have to be properly managed by senior executives and overseen by the board as an expression of the duty of care (OECD, 2020, pp. 74-75[66]), regardless of any more complex discussion about the scope of the duty of loyalty.

## 2.6. Shareholders' rights

Corporate and securities laws usually provide – in a language similar to the one adopted by G20/OECD Principle II – that shareholders have the right to "obtain relevant and material information on the corporation on a timely and regular basis", "elect and remove members of the board", and "approve or participate in decisions concerning fundamental corporate changes". As seen in Section 1.7, shareholders have been exercising some of those rights on matters related to climate change, such as requesting a company to substantially reduce Scope 3 GHG emissions. Likewise, investors managing more than USD 10 trillion have reported to be willing to engage with companies on sustainability issues (see Table 1.2).

What may not be clear in some jurisdictions and in the G20/OECD Principles are the limits for a majority of shareholders to impose non-financial goals and reporting obligations to companies (especially public ones). Arguably the two rights are closely linked: if the central objective of the corporation is to maximise long-term shareholder value, the relevant information to be disclosed would be focused on what is financially material. However, when the corporation has societal or environmental goals together with the purpose of maximising shareholders' wealth, both what is financially material and relevant to those chosen non-financial goals may need to be reported to shareholders.

This section will refer to the discussion on materiality above, and focus on the questions related to the imposition by shareholders of non-financial objectives that would divert a company from the sole purpose of making profits. Under any circumstance, the following should be clear: if the fulfilment of a stakeholder's interest is expected to increase a company's long-term value, it is beyond doubt that management should be allowed to fulfil such an interest. The hard question – which is the focus of the following paragraphs – is whether a trade-off between long-term value and stakeholders' interests may be possible.

Something to consider is that some individuals who are – directly or through investment vehicles[32] – shareholders of listed companies are also philanthropists and may have concerns other than their wealth. Even mainstream economic models that assume rational behaviour often recognise that individuals maximise their utility, which may include avoiding an environmental catastrophe, and not strictly their wealth. This begs the question of whether corporations should fulfil their shareholders' willingness to advance the common good instead of distributing dividends that may be eventually donated by the shareholders to philanthropic institutions.

It is difficult to assess the extent to which individuals would accept a trade-off between their wealth and public goods. A proxy may be the value of assets under management by philanthropic foundations, which are sometimes linked to controlling shareholders or founders of public companies, in 24 major jurisdictions in all continents: USD 1.5 trillion in assets as of mid-2010s with an annual average expenditure rate of 10% (Johnson, 2018, pp. 17-20[67]). These assets under management represent only around 1% of global equity markets, which may signal that individuals' willingness to accept an exchange of their wealth for public goods is low.

Despite its conceivable small practical relevance as suggested in the paragraph above, it may be argued that corporations could provide some public goods (or reduce a public bad) more cost-effectively than philanthropic institutions. For instance, permits for European companies to emit one ton of $CO_2$ (a proxy of the cost for a company to emit one less ton) reached a record price of USD 71 in August 2021 (Financial Times, 2021[68]) while the cost of capturing $CO_2$ directly in the air (what an independent institution may do) – without even considering the costs of transporting and storing it – was over USD 134 a tonne in 2019 (Baylin-Stern and Berghout, 2021[69]). In many other contexts, however, corporations may not have any clear advantage in advancing the common good when compared to philanthropic institutions, such as if a fossil fuel company were to develop a reforestation project.

In considering the challenges above, a majority of shareholders have the right in some jurisdictions to eventually decide to change a company's articles of association in order to establish goals other than maximising long-term value. That is exactly what – as detailed in Section 1.7 – shareholders may do in Delaware with the PBCs and in France with the *sociétés à mission*. In those cases, however, some consideration may also be due to the rights of shareholders that opposed the transformation in the purpose of the corporation. After all, in many jurisdictions, shareholders have traditionally had at least a *de facto* expectation that the main goal of a company is to maximise long-term value. For instance, jurisdictions could consider the advantages and drawbacks of requiring a supermajority to add non-financial goals, or the right for dissenting shareholders to sell their shares back to the corporation at a fair price.

Finally, companies that voluntarily adopt environmental and social goals will face the challenge of making directors and key executives accountable both for their financial and non-financial performance. As previously mentioned in the "directors' fiduciary duties" subsection, since the comparison between goals of different natures can be difficult, companies may consider adopting new controls, such as hiring an independent third-party to regularly verify whether management fulfilled its non-financial goals. Governments may even decide to regulate which controls must be adopted in case a company voluntarily assumes non-financial goals in order to protect the interests of retail investors and unsophisticated stakeholders who value the company higher due to its commitment to the environment and society.

## 2.7. Financing climate transition

On top of governance related challenges discussed in this report, it is crucial that policy makers also address the issues related to the financing of the climate transition. The Paris Agreement stresses the necessity of financing the climate change transition as one of its three long-term goals. In Article 2.1.c, the Parties committed to "make finance flows consistent with a pathway towards low greenhouse gas emissions and climate-resilient development" (UN, 2015[3]).

As set out in Section 1.5, almost 65% of listed companies globally face financially material risks in terms of Scope 1 and Scope 2 GHG emissions, as well as the physical impact of climate change. While it is clear that mobilising a major amount of funds is necessary to finance the activities for the adaptation to and mitigation of climate risks faced by those companies, the exact amount of funds required is uncertain. According to one estimate, a USD 6.9 trillion investment for 15 years between 2015 and 2030 would be needed to meet climate objectives in the infrastructure industry in line with the Paris Agreement (OECD, 2017[70]). Another estimate for the energy industry claims that annual clean energy investment worldwide will need to more than triple by 2030 to around USD 4 trillion to reach net zero emissions by 2050 (IEA, 2021[71]). At the regional level, financing the net zero GHG emissions target of the EU by 2050 is estimated to cost an annual investment of 2% of GDP of which public investment would amount to between 0.5 and 1% of GDP (Darvas and Wolff, 2021[72]).

Public resources alone will not be enough to cover the trillions of dollars needed to fulfil the goals of the Paris Agreement, and to adapt infrastructure and industrial systems to climate change. Private financing sources such as institutional investors will also have a key role to play in financing the climate transition. Recently, sovereign and corporate green bonds have been issued in response to demands for climate finance, even though the spreads on ESG corporate bonds versus their conventional counterparts has been often negligible (Stubbington, 2021[73]). Since the first green bond issued in 2007, there has been a gradual increase in the amount of funds raised via green bonds, reaching almost USD 300 billion in2020 (CBI, 2021[74]), which is still a modest amount compared to the USD 18 trillion of government borrowing by OECD countries (OECD, 2021[75]) as well as the USD 5.9 trillion in corporate bond borrowing the same year.[33] The criteria for determining whether an activity to be financed by the issuance of a corporate bond is environmentally sustainable, however, can vary. In order to protect the buyers of corporate bonds and other financial instruments, some jurisdictions have been developing a taxonomy to classify which economic activities could be considered environmentally sustainable (allowing, for instance, a company to name a bond it issues as "green").[34]

The establishment of an emissions trading system is one among different policies jurisdictions may use to create market-based incentives to reduce carbon emissions where these are more cost-effective. In most compliance trading systems, the government sets an emissions ceiling for companies in high-polluting sectors, and corporates covered by the system may trade emissions permits – buying if they want to emit more than what they are allowed, or selling permits if they emit less (IEA, 2020[76]). Voluntary carbon credit markets may also allow entities not covered by emission ceilings to manage their carbon footprint or to raise private financing for projects with positive contributions for the climate transition (TSVCM, 2021[77]). For instance, a company with a self-imposed target of net zero emissions may decide to acquire carbon credits if they are (at the margin) cheaper than reducing its own carbon emissions. Likewise, municipalities or private entities may be able to sell carbon credits representing effective reductions in their emissions (e.g. avoided deforestation) or carbon captured in their projects (e.g. technology-based removal). For a system of carbon credits or permits to work efficiently, however, the certification of emissions reduction and carbon captured must be credible (just like external auditors and custodians are needed for a stock market to flourish) and flows of negotiation should be as free as feasible (so that carbon emission reductions are achieved for the smallest possible costs). Standardisation of carbon credits is especially important to facilitate trading flows, making cross-border negotiations and price-discovery easier.

Policy makers can contribute to the climate transition by creating policies and a regulatory environment that leverage the necessary private finance. In this respect, it is important to identify the degree of the contribution to climate action by each financing type so that policy makers can direct their efforts to increase the efficiency of financing towards climate goals. Empirical evidence shows that economies with relatively more funding from stock markets than from credit markets generate fewer carbon emissions. Even within carbon-intensive sectors, more developed stock markets are associated with more green patents. Importantly, the size of financial markets alone – independent of the size of stock markets -- is not related to the environmental performance of the economy (Haas and Popov, 2019[78]).

The positive contribution of stock markets to a greener economy comes from their critical role in supporting innovation through equity investors' willingness to share the risk in projects to a higher proportion of intangibles assets. Deeper stock markets are found to enable the growth of innovative sectors with less tangible assets such as energy efficient sectors, while sectors with more tangible assets that are higher carbon emitters, grow faster in economies that depend more on bank financing (Brown, Martinsson and Petersen, 2017[79]). Moreover, equity investors' demand and power in pushing companies towards greener technologies may contribute to stock markets' better performance in terms of financing climate reduction, as shareholders mostly want to decrease any future cost for the company of the management of environmental risks such as compliance and litigation costs, fines, penalties, and reputational damage. On top of that, private equity and venture capital have the potential to strengthen the positive impact of stock markets on climate action through their support for innovative high-tech risky start-ups that lack the scale to access public markets. To a certain extent, the discussion between financing of innovation and risk appetite of investors also holds for the corporate bond market, as longer term corporate bonds can be used to finance longer term innovative projects that could support the climate transition. Additionally, investors in corporate bonds, not necessarily green ones, can, through provisions on covenants, also use their stakeholder powers to drive companies' green transformation.[35]

# 3 Recent regulatory developments

This chapter presents recent climate-related regulatory initiatives and proposals advanced by OECD, G20 and FSB members for their corporate governance frameworks, with a particular focus on corporate disclosure. It first summarises the status of agreements among international groupings and organisations such as the G20, G7, the Financial Stability Board and IOSCO. The chapter then describes in detail some of the more significant recent national initiatives to strengthen climate-related disclosure, undertaken notably by many G20 and FSB members, a number of large OECD economies and by the European Union.

Recent regulatory initiatives and proposals by OECD, G20 and FSB members suggest both a growing focus on and emerging consensus around many aspects of ESG and climate change, notably with respect to disclosure. This section focuses particularly on disclosure, as it is the area where most regulatory adjustments have been made recently. This consensus is also reflected in recent reports and statements of international groupings and organisations.

In their July 2021 Communiqué, **G20 Finance Ministers and Central Bank Governors** pledged "to promote implementation of disclosure requirements or guidance, building on the FSB's Task Force on Climate-related Financial Disclosures (TCFD) framework, in line with domestic regulatory frameworks, to pave the way for future global co-ordination efforts, taking into account jurisdictions' circumstances, aimed at developing a baseline global reporting standard. To that aim, [the G20] welcome[s] the work programme of the International Financial Reporting Standards Foundation to develop a baseline global reporting standard under robust governance and public oversight, building upon the TCFD framework and the work of sustainability standard-setters, involving them and consulting with a wide range of stakeholders to foster global best practices".

In their October 2021 Communiqué, G20 Finance Ministers and Central Bank Governors endorsed the G20 **Sustainable Finance Roadmap** prepared by the G20 Sustainable Finance Working Group (SFWG). The Roadmap, initially focused on climate, is a multi-year action-oriented document that is voluntary and flexible in nature (G20, 2021[80]). The SFWG roadmap includes 19 actions on sustainable finance to be undertaken by different international organisations. Focus areas include market development and approaches to align investments to sustainability goals; consistent, comparable, and decision-useful information on sustainability; and assessment and management of climate and other sustainability risks.

**The statement of the G7 Leaders** meeting of 11-13 June 2021 states that "We support moving towards mandatory climate-related financial disclosures that provide consistent and decision-useful information for market participants and that are based on the Task Force on Climate-related Financial Disclosures (TCFD) framework, in line with domestic regulatory frameworks." Likewise, the **Financial Stability Board**, comprised of G20 Members plus Hong Kong (**China**), the Netherlands, Singapore, Spain, Switzerland has also endorsed the TCFD framework as a basis for promoting such comparable standards globally.

The FSB's report on Promoting Climate-Related Disclosure reveals that regulation and guidance related to this issue is evolving extremely rapidly (FSB, 2021[81]). The report indicates that 14 out of its 25 members already have requirements or guidance in place for climate-related disclosures.[36] While not providing an overall tally of the number of jurisdictions that make such reporting mandatory versus voluntary, the report does further indicate that 21 of the 25 FSB members have either already established or plan to establish requirements or guidance on climate-related disclosure for both publicly listed corporations and financial institutions. Twelve of the 21 jurisdictions with such existing or planned provisions also intend to apply them to non-listed corporations. Another three jurisdictions indicated they have plans to develop such standards for financial institutions only, while only one reported having no such plans for either group.

**The International Organization of Securities Commissions (IOSCO)** established a Sustainable Finance Task Force (STF) in April 2020 which issued a Report on Sustainability-related Issuer Disclosures (2021[58]) calling for strengthened sustainability reporting with an initial focus on climate-related issues. Following a survey focusing on investors' needs and the current status of corporate disclosures on sustainability, the Task Force concluded "that investor demand for sustainability-related information is currently not being properly met [..]. Accordingly, in February 2021, the IOSCO Board concluded that there is an urgent need to work towards improving the completeness, consistency, comparability, reliability and auditability of sustainability reporting – including greater emphasis on industry-specific quantitative metrics and standardisation of narrative information."

The findings of the IOSCO report are intended to serve as input to the IFRS Foundation's work to establish the International Sustainability Standards Board (ISSB) to develop a baseline global sustainability reporting standard. The report also strongly encourages the ISSB "to leverage the content of existing sustainability-related reporting principles, frameworks and guidance, including the TCFD's recommendations, as it develops investor-oriented standards focused on enterprise value, beginning with climate change." Moreover, IOSCO encouraged a "building blocks" approach, meaning that a global sustainability standard should provide flexibility for complementary standards serving stakeholders and applying definitions of materiality that are broader than what is financially material. From a practical point of view, in March 2021 IOSCO established a Technical Experts Group under its STF to undertake an assessment of the technical recommendations to be developed by the ISSB (IOSCO, 2021[82]).

The following paragraphs describe some of the more significant national regulatory initiatives to strengthen climate-related disclosure across OECD, G20 and FSB jurisdictions. Among these, a number of jurisdictions have so far focused on prioritising climate-related reporting based on traditionally applied concepts of materiality, the approach followed by the TCFD.

In 2010, the **US** SEC provided an interpretive release for issuers as to how existing disclosure requirements apply to climate change matters (SEC, 2010[83]). This 2010 guidance noted that, depending on the circumstances, information about climate-related risks and opportunities might be required in a company's disclosures related to its description of business, legal proceedings, risk factors, and management's discussion and analysis of financial condition and results of operations.

In June 2021, the SEC announced that the "disclosure relating to climate risk, human capital, including workforce diversity and corporate board diversity, and cybersecurity risk" would be in its annual regulatory agenda (US SEC, 2021[84]). In September 2021 SEC staff published a sample letter to companies regarding climate change disclosures in line with the abovementioned 2010 guidance, presenting comments companies may need to consider (US SEC, 2021[85]). For instance, those sample comments include the following: "disclose any material litigation risks related to climate change and explain the potential impact to the company", and "to the extent material, discuss the indirect consequences of climate-related regulation or business trends".

In March 2022, the SEC proposed "rule changes that would require registrants to include certain climate-related disclosures in their registration statements and periodic reports, including information about climate-related risks that are reasonably likely to have a material impact on their business, results of operations, or financial condition, and certain climate-related financial statement metrics in a note to their audited financial statements. The required information about climate-related risks also would include disclosure of a registrant's greenhouse gas emissions" (SEC, 2022[86]).

In **Japan**, the Financial Services Agency (JFSA) issued, in June 2021, a revised Corporate Governance Code to include requirements for companies listed in Japan's Prime Market to disclose climate-related information based on the TCFD recommendations on a "comply or explain" basis (FSB, 2021[81]). In particular, the amended Corporate Governance Code suggests that companies "should collect and analyse the necessary data on the impact of climate change-related risks and earnings opportunities on their business activities and profits, and enhance the quality and quantity of disclosure based on the TCFD recommendations, which are an internationally well-established disclosure framework, or an equivalent framework."

During the JFSA's public consultation on the revision of the code, the agency explained that the IFRS Foundation is in the process of developing a unified disclosure framework for sustainability, while taking into account the TCFD recommendations, and that "it is expected that the framework will be equivalent to the TCFD recommendations."

To promote implementation, the JFSA together with the Ministry of Economy, Trade and Industry, and the Ministry of the Environment have supported the foundation of the TCFD Foundation Consortium of Japan, which comprises 350 companies and has provided a platform to support and develop more detailed supplemental guidance to help companies comply with TCFD recommendations (TCFD, 2021, p. 25[15]).

Japan's Stewardship Code, amended in 2020, explicitly instructs institutional investors to consider, in the context of constructive engagement with investees, the medium to long-term sustainability aspects, including ESG factors, according to their investment strategies. While neither the Corporate Governance Code nor the Stewardship Code specifically recommend the establishment of a board or management sustainability committee, Japan's revised "Guidelines for Investor and Company Engagement" raise a series of questions for investor and company consideration that ask whether the company has a structure in place to review and promote sustainability-related initiatives on an enterprise-wide basis.

In the **United Kingdom**, all listed companies must report – since the enactment of the 2006 Companies Act – the annual quantity of Scopes 1 and 2 $CO_2$ emissions, as well as an expression of the company's total annual emissions in relation to a proxy of the size of its activities (i.e. the energy intensity). More recently, under the Green Finance Strategy, the United Kingdom established a TCFD Task Force which convened relevant government and regulatory institutions to develop a 2020 interim report and "A roadmap towards mandatory climate-related disclosures". The interim report describes a phased and multi-pronged approach to delivering TCFD-aligned disclosures by 2025. The roadmap sets out indicative measures to be taken by government and regulators and an indicative implementation path across multiple types of organisations, including for listed commercial companies and financial institutions.

In the case of listed companies, the UK Financial Conduct Authority (FCA) introduced a Listing Rule for premium listed companies in January 2021 referencing the TCFD recommendations and associated guidance.[37] Premium listed companies that have not made fully consistent TCFD-aligned disclosures should explain why they have not done so and set out any steps they are taking or plan to take to be able to make such disclosures in the future, as well as the timeframe within which they expect to be able to make consistent disclosures. The FCA also initiated a consultation in June 2021 on extending this requirement to a wider scope of listed companies beginning on 1 January 2022 (FSB, 2021, p. 10[81]).

Additionally, the UK FCA – which has six remuneration codes covering different kinds of regulated financial services firms[38] – recently wrote to the remuneration committee chairs of companies covered by these codes, stating that the FCA expects them to include ESG factors within directors' remuneration. Likewise, the latest remuneration code enacted by the FCA[39] explicitly states that firms should consider ESG factors when setting remuneration policies and practices (UK FCA, 2022[87]).

The UK's Department for Business, Energy and Industrial Strategy (BEIS) has also undertaken a consultation, and the government announced in October 2021 that the UK's largest traded companies, banks, insurers and private companies with over 500 employees and GBP 500 million in turnover will have to disclose climate-related information in line with the TCFD recommendations from April 2022 onwards, which will include over 1 300 businesses (UK Department for Business, Energy and Industrial Strategy, 2021[88]).

The **European Union** is taking a broad approach both to ESG and climate change-focused reporting. The Non-Financial Reporting Directive (NFRD),[40] which took effect in 2018, includes non-binding guidelines that reference the TCFD recommendations for climate-related disclosures. The NFRD includes ESG disclosure requirements for large companies to publish information related not only to environmental matters, but also to social matters such as the treatment of employees.

An analysis of current NFRD implementation reviewing 1 000 European companies' sustainability reports undertaken by the Alliance for Corporate Transparency found "a marked gap between what companies say about climate change and support for the TCFD, and their actual reporting practice" (2019[89]). The report concluded that most companies fail to report on targets on climate change, even in the energy sector where climate-related reporting is farthest advanced, while the vast majority of companies fail to have specific risk mitigation strategies. Although the TCFD recommends that companies provide clear information and metrics on climate risks and how they are being addressed, the report found that overall, less than 32% of all companies reported on such a strategy, while only 23% addressed specific climate risks.

With this implementation gap in mind, the European Commission published in 2021 a proposal for a Corporate Sustainability Reporting Directive (CSRD) (European Commission, 2021[90]) that would further extend such requirements both in relation to climate as well as information on intangibles such as intellectual capital and human capital.

The EU April 2021 CSRD proposal, among other provisions, would:

- extend the scope of disclosure requirements from certain large public interest companies to all large companies and all companies listed on regulated markets except micro-enterprises[41]
- require the assurance of reported information based on a "limited" rather than a more demanding "reasonable" assurance requirement (currently, there is no requirement for a third-party review)
- include more detailed due diligence reporting requirements, taking into account internationally recognised principles and frameworks on responsible business conduct including the OECD Guidelines for Multinational Enterprises

- introduce more detailed reporting requirements according to mandatory EU sustainability reporting standards to be developed by the European Financial Reporting Advisory Group (EFRAG) in the form of technical advice. These requirements would encompass the need to disclose not just the risks to companies but also the impacts of companies on society and the environment, i.e. the "double materiality" principle.

In April 2019, the European Parliament adopted an EU Regulation for Sustainability-related Disclosures in the Financial Services Sector which took effect in March 2021. The Regulation calls on financial institutions to disclose sustainability risks and impacts and encourages financial institutions to take into account impacts to both society and the environment. Specifically, the regulation introduces transparency rules for financial institutions on the integration of sustainability risks and impacts in their processes and financial products, including reporting on adherence to internationally recognised standards for due diligence.[42]

In February 2022, the European Commission published a proposal for a Directive on Corporate Sustainability Due Diligence (European Commission, 2022[91]), which aims at:

- improving corporate governance practices to better integrate risk management and mitigation processes of human rights and environmental risks and impacts, including those stemming from value chains, into corporate strategies
- avoiding fragmentation of due diligence requirements in the single market and create legal certainty for businesses and stakeholders as regards expected behaviour and liability
- increasing corporate accountability for adverse impacts, and ensuring coherence for companies regarding obligations under existing and proposed EU initiatives on responsible business conduct
- improving access to remedies for those affected by adverse human rights and environmental impacts of corporate behaviour.

**France** is another early adopter of ESG disclosure requirements on the social and environmental consequences of corporate activities, established under the Grenelle II Law enacted in 2010. These requirements were further strengthened and became more climate-focused in 2015 with the enactment of the French Energy Transition Law,[43] which imposed new requirements for listed companies to disclose their financial risks related to the effects of climate change and the measures adopted by the company to reduce them. The Energy Transition Law also established requirements for banks and credit institutions to disclose the results of stress tests that take into consideration climate-related risks, and instituted new requirements for institutional investors to disclose information on how ESG criteria are considered in their investment decisions and how their policies align with the national strategy for energy and ecological transition. France's 2017 law on the Duty of Vigilance places a due diligence duty on large French companies and requires them to publish an annual "vigilance plan". Plans must outline measures related to both human rights and environmental risks and adverse impacts.[44]

The **German** Sustainability Code provides a voluntary sustainability reporting standard for any type of company, including the recommendation for companies to disclose their GHG emissions in accordance with the GHG Protocol and to communicate their goals to reduce GHG emissions (German Council for Sustainable Development, 2018, p. 47[92]). In Germany, companies in which the national Government has a majority holding, which have more than 500 employees and which achieve an annual turnover of over EUR 500 million must disclose a sustainability report in line with either the German Sustainability Code or a comparable framework for sustainability reporting.

Between October 2021 and February 2022, **Canada**'s national body representing provincial and territorial securities administrators held a public consultation proposing to put in place requirements to improve the consistency and comparability of information issuers disclose to investors for them to make investment decisions. The disclosure requirements contemplated are largely consistent with TCFD recommendations. In December 2021, the Canadian Prime Minister directed the ministers of Environment and Climate Change and of Finance to work with Canada's provinces and territories to move toward mandatory climate-related financial disclosures based on TCFD's framework and to require federally regulated institutions, including financial institutions and pension funds, to issue climate-related financial disclosures and net zero plans.

**Australia**'s national corporate governance code requires listed companies to report in an annual corporate governance statement on whether they have any material exposure to environmental and social risks under the code's recommendation 7.4,[45] which must be followed on a "comply or explain" basis. The Australian Council of Superannuation Investors (ACSI) and the Financial Services Council (FSC) also issued a more detailed ESG Reporting Guide for Australian Companies in 2015.

In the **People's Republic of China (hereafter 'China'),** the China Securities Regulatory Commission (CSRC) issued new rules in June 2021 amending environmental and social disclosure requirements for listed companies. Annual and semi-annual reports will now need to consolidate environmental and social information under *Section 5: Environmental and Social Responsibility*. These will include mandatory disclosure for certain "key polluting companies" on pollutant emissions, while other non-key companies will follow a "comply or explain" regime for such disclosures.[46] Companies will also be encouraged to voluntarily disclose relevant information related to other environmental measures, including the reduction of carbon emissions. Other voluntary provisions relate to company efforts in fulfilling their social responsibility including, but not limited to, the protection of the rights and interests of employees, suppliers, customers and consumers, poverty alleviation and rural revitalisation.

In **Hong Kong (China)**, the various financial and supervisory authorities have established a target to develop TCFD-aligned disclosure standards across all relevant sectors by 2025. The Hong Kong Exchanges and Clearing Limited (HKEX) has already issued new ESG reporting requirements effective from July 2020 which incorporate certain elements of the TCFD recommendations, while "encouraging" issuers to adopt the TCFD recommendations more fully (FSB, 2021[81]).

In **India**, the Securities and Exchange Board (SEBI) issued a circular in May 2021 implementing new sustainability-related reporting requirements for the top 1 000 listed companies by market capitalisation (SEBI, 2021[93]). New disclosure will be made in the format of the Business Responsibility and Sustainability Report (BRSR), which builds upon SEBI's existing Business Responsibility Report and is intended to bring sustainability reporting up to existing financial reporting standards.[47] Disclosure will be voluntary in FY 2021-22 and mandatory for the first time in FY 2022-23.

The BRSR format is based on the nine principles of the Indian Government's "National Guidelines on Responsible Business Conduct" (Government of India, 2018[94]), and sets out metrics under each principle, divided into mandatory essential indicators, and leadership indicators, which operate on a voluntary basis. In addition to an overall directive to provide an overview of the company's material ESG risks and opportunities and approach to mitigate or adapt to the risks, together with relevant financial implications, the circular sets out five types of more specific indicators that companies should report on in connection with the principle to respect and make efforts to protect and restore the environment. These include:

- Resource usage (energy and water) and intensity metrics
- Air pollutant emissions
- Greenhouse gas emissions (Scope 1, Scope 2 and Scope 3)
- Waste generated and waste management practices
- Impact on bio-diversity

The **Singapore** Exchange (SGX) has introduced a mandatory sustainability disclosure regime beginning from FY 2022, which covers climate-related risks among other ESG issues. The climate-related reporting rules mandated by the SGX requires issuers to follow a "phased approach" in accordance with the industries identified by TCFD as most affected by climate change and the transition to a lower-carbon economy. In 2022 all issuers are required to adopt the reporting rules on a "comply or explain" basis; in

2023 it will be mandatory for issuers in the (i) financial, (ii) agriculture, food and forest products, and (iii) energy industries; and in 2024 for issuers in the (i) materials and buildings, and (ii) transportation industries.

In **Indonesia**, the Financial Services Authority (OJK), as part of efforts to create a financial system that applies sustainable principles, introduced a rule in 2017 that requires financial services providers, issuers and public companies to implement sustainable finance in their business activities. In this context, sustainable finance is defined by OJK Rule 51 as comprehensive support from financial services sector to create sustainable economic growth by harmonising economic, social and environmental interests. Effective implementation date of the Rule differs by size and business classification of the entities (the earliest in 2019 for commercial banks and the latest by 2025 for pension funds). The Rule calls for the earliest possible implementation by issuers and publicly listed companies (OJK, 2021[95]).

In September 2021, the Central Bank of **Brazil** announced mandatory disclosure aligned with the TCFD recommendations for financial institutions (BCB, 2021[96]). In a first phase, the rule will require the disclosure of qualitative aspects related to governance, strategy and risk management, and, in a second phase, quantitative information will also be required. In December 2021, the Securities and Exchange Commission of Brazil (CVM) amended its main rule governing issuers' disclosure, adding new requirements to increase transparency of ESG-related issues. The rule follows mostly a "comply or explain" approach with emphasis on climate-related requirements, but it also introduces disclosure requirements related to other ESG aspects, such as workforce and board diversity. Disclosures will become mandatory from January 2023 onwards and apply to 2022 annual filings.

In **Chile**, the Financial Market Commission issued in November 2021 regulation that integrates sustainability and corporate governance issues into the annual report of issuers of publicly traded securities, banks, insurance companies, general fund managers and financial market infrastructures (CMF, 2021[97]). The regulation requires the disclosure of policies and indicators on some ESG factors, including climate change, based on international standards such as Integrated Reporting, GRI and TCFD. In addition, the regulation requires that issuers of publicly traded securities, banks and insurance companies report industry-specific material metrics in accordance with the SASB standards. The regulation will come into force gradually depending on the type of entity and its size in terms of consolidated assets, starting with the 2022 annual report up to 2024.

# References


Alliance for Corporate Transparency (2019), *2019 Reserach Report*, https://www.allianceforcorporatetransparency.org/assets/2019_Research_Report%20_Alliance_for_Corporate_Transparency.pdf. [89]

Anderson, N. (2019), *IFRS® Standards and climate-related disclosures*, https://cdn.ifrs.org/content/dam/ifrs/news/2019/november/in-brief-climate-change-nick-anderson.pdf?la=en. [52]

As You Sow (2021), *Proxy Preview 2021*, https://www.proxyimpact.com/publications. [34]

As You Sow (2021), *Record Breaking Year for Environmental, Social, and Sustainable Governance Shareholder Resolutions*, https://www.asyousow.org/press-releases/2021/6/24/record-breaking-year-for-environmental-social-and-sustainable-governance-shareholder-resolutions. [35]

Baylin-Stern, A. and N. Berghout (2021), *Is carbon capture too expensive?*, https://www.iea.org/commentaries/is-carbon-capture-too-expensive. [69]

BCB (2021), *New regulation on social, environmental, and climate-related risk disclosures*, https://www.bcb.gov.br/content/about/legislation_norms_docs/BCB_Disclosure-GRSAC-Report.pdf. [96]

Bebchuk, L. (2021), "Don't Let the Short-Termism Bogeyman Scare You", *Harvard Business Review* January–February 2021, https://hbr.org/2021/01/dont-let-the-short-termism-bogeyman-scare-you. [43]

Belsom, T. and L. Lake (2021), *ESG factors and equity returns – a review of recent industry research*, https://www.unpri.org/pri-blog/esg-factors-and-equity-returns-a-review-of-recent-industry-research/7867.article (accessed on  September 2021). [22]

Boffo, R. and R. Patalano (2020), *ESG Investing: Practices, Progress and Challenges*, OECD Paris, https://www.oecd.org/finance/ESG-Investing-Practices-Progress-and-Challenges.pdf. [24]

BP (2020), *Annual Report and Form 20-F 2020*, https://www.bp.com/content/dam/bp/business-sites/en/global/corporate/pdfs/investors/bp-annual-report-and-form-20f-2020.pdf. [51]

Brown, J., G. Martinsson and B. Petersen (2017), "Stock markets, credit markets, and technology-led growth", *Journal of Financial Intermediation*, pp. 45-59. [79]

Busch, T. and G. Friede (2018), *The Robustness of the Corporate Social and Financial Performance Relation: A Second-Order Meta-Analysis*. [100]

Business Roundtable (2019), *Statement on the Purpose of a Corporation*, https://s3.amazonaws.com/brt.org/BRT- [29]

StatementonthePurposeofaCorporationJuly2021.pdf.

CBI (2021), *Green Bond Pricing in the Primary Market: January - June 2021.* [74]

CDSB (2019), *CDSB Framework for reporting environmental & climate change information*, https://www.cdsb.net/what-we-do/reporting-frameworks/environmental-information-natural-capital. [13]

Ceres (2021), *In historic votes, shareholders demand strong climate action from the U.S. oil and gas industry*, https://www.ceres.org/news-center/press-releases/historic-votes-shareholders-demand-strong-climate-action-us-oil-and-gas (accessed on 23 August 2021). [36]

Chalmers, J., E. Cox and N. Picard (2021), *The economic realities of ESG*, https://www.pwc.com/gx/en/services/audit-assurance/corporate-reporting/esg-investor-survey.html. [60]

Climate Action 100+ (2021), *Initiative Snapshot*, https://www.climateaction100.org/ (accessed on 20 December 2021). [105]

CMF (2021), *Norma de Caráter General n. 461*, https://www.cmfchile.cl/normativa/ncg_461_2021.pdf. [97]

Corporate Reporting Dialogue (2019), *Driving Alignment in Climate-related Reporting*, https://corporatereportingdialogue.com/publication/driving-alignment-in-climate-related-reporting/. [17]

Darvas, Z. and G. Wolff (2021), *A green fiscal pact: climate investment in times of budget consolidation.* [72]

European Commission (2022), *Proposal for a Directive on corporate sustainability due diligence*, https://ec.europa.eu/info/publications/proposal-directive-corporate-sustainable-due-diligence-and-annex_en. [91]

European Commission (2021), *Proposal for a Directive of teh European Parliament and of the Council as regards corporate sustainability reporting*, https://eur-lex.europa.eu/legal-content/EN/TXT/HTML/?uri=CELEX:52021PC0189&from=EN. [90]

FASB (2021), *FASB Staff Educational Paper: Intersection of Environmental, Social and Governance M atters with Financial Accounting Standards*, https://www.fasb.org/Page/ShowPdf?path=FASB_Staff_ESG_Educational_Paper_FINAL.pdf. [50]

Feldman, N. et al. (2018), "The Long and Short of It: Do Public and Private Firms Invest Differently?", *Federal Reserve Board Finance and Economics Discussion Series*, http://www.federalreserve.gov/econres/feds/files/2018068pap.pdf. [49]

Financial Times (2021), *Carbon price rises above €60 to set new record*, https://www.ft.com/content/c1a78427-f3d5-4b4f-9878-c3e1dffee2ba. [68]

Fink, L. (2020), *A Fundamental Reshaping of Finance*, https://www.blackrock.com/corporate/investor-relations/2020-larry-fink-ceo-letter. [30]

Fisch, J. and S. Davidoff Solomon (2021), "Should Corporations have a Purpose?", *Texas Law Review, Vol. 99, p. 1309, 2021, U of Penn, Inst for Law & Econ Research Paper No. 20-22, European Corporate Governance Institute - Law Working Paper No. 510/2020,* [32] https://papers.ssrn.com/sol3/papers.cfm?abstract_id=3561164.

Freshfields (2021), *A Legal Framework for Impact*, https://www.freshfields.com/en-gb/our-thinking/campaigns/a-legal-framework-for-impact/. [108]

Friedman, M. (1970), *The Social Responsibility Of Business Is to Increase Its Profits*, https://www.nytimes.com/1970/09/13/archives/a-friedman-doctrine-the-social-responsibility-of-business-is-to.html. [28]

FSB (2021), *Report on promoting climate-related disclosures*, https://www.fsb.org/2021/07/report-on-promoting-climate-related-disclosures/. [81]

G&A Institute (2020), *Trends on the sustainability reporting practices of S&P Index companies*, https://www.ga-institute.com/research-reports/flash-reports/2020-sp-500-flash-report.html. [16]

G20 (2021), *G20 Sustainable Finance Roadmap*, https://g20sfwg.org/wp-content/uploads/2021/10/G20-Sustainable-Finance-Roadmap.pdf. [80]

German Council for Sustainable Development (2018), *The Sustainability Code*, https://www.deutscher-nachhaltigkeitskodex.de/de-DE/Documents/PDFs/Sustainability-Code-(1)/SustainabilityCode_brochure_2020_A5_EN.aspx. [92]

GIIN, G. (2020), *Annual Impact Investor Survey 2020*, https://thegiin.org/research/publication/impinv-survey-2020. [98]

Gosling, T. et al. (2021), *Paying well by paying for good*, PWC. [25]

Government of India (2018), *National Guidelines on Responsible Business Conduct*, https://www.mca.gov.in/Ministry/pdf/NationalGuildeline_15032019.pdf. [94]

GSI (2020), *Global Sustainable Investment Review*, http://www.gsi-alliance.org/. [109]

GSI Alliance, G. (2021), *Global Sustainable Investment Review 2020*, http://www.gsi-alliance.org/. [8]

Gutiérrez, G. and T. Philippon (2016), “Investment-less Growth: An Empirical Investigation”, *NBER Working Paper Series*, http://www.nber.org/system/files/working_papers/w22897/w22897.pdf. [48]

Haas, R. and A. Popov (2019), “Finance and decarbonisation: why equity markets do it better”, *Research Bulletin No:64*. [78]

IAASB (2020), *The Consideration of Climate-Related Risks in an Audit of Financial Statement*, https://www.ifac.org/system/files/publications/files/IAASB-Climate-Audit-Practice-Alert.pdf. [53]

IAASB (2013), *ISAE 3000 (Revised), Assurance Engagements Other than Audits or Reviews of Historical Financial Information*, https://www.ifac.org/system/files/publications/files/ISAE 3000 Revised - for IAASB.pdf. [101]

IAASB (2000), *International Framework for Assurance Engagements*, https://www.iaasb.org/projects/assurance-engagements-completed. [104]

IASB (2018), *Conceptual Framework for Financial Reporting*, https://www.ifrs.org/issued-standards/list-of-standards/conceptual-framework.html. [14]

IEA (2021), *Net Zero 2050: A Roadmap for the Global Energy Sector*, [71] https://iea.blob.core.windows.net/assets/beceb956-0dcf-4d73-89fe-1310e3046d68/NetZeroby2050-ARoadmapfortheGlobalEnergySector_CORR.pdf.

IEA (2020), *Implementing Effective Emissions Trading Systems: Lessons from international experiences*, https://www.iea.org/reports/implementing-effective-emissions-trading-systems. [76]

IEA, I. (2021), *Net Zero by 2050 A Roadmap for the Global Energy Sector*, http://www.iea.org/t&c/. [7]

IFAC and AICPA (2021), *The State of Play in Sustainability Assurance*, https://www.ifac.org/knowledge-gateway/contributing-global-economy/discussion/state-play-sustainability-assurance. [19]

IFRS Foundation (2021), *IFRS Foundation announces International Sustainability Standards Board, consolidation with CDSB and VRF, and publication of prototype disclosure requirements*, https://www.ifrs.org/news-and-events/news/2021/11/ifrs-foundation-announces-issb-consolidation-with-cdsb-vrf-publication-of-prototypes/ (accessed on 23 December 2021). [64]

IFRS Foundation (2021), *Proposed Targeted Amendments to the IFRS Foundation Constitution to Accommodate an International Sustainability Standards Board to Set IFRS Sustainability Standards*, https://www.ifrs.org/content/dam/ifrs/project/sustainability-reporting/ed-2021-5-proposed-constitution-amendments-to-accommodate-sustainability-board.pdf. [65]

IFRS Foundation (2018), *Who uses IFRS Standards?*, https://www.ifrs.org/use-around-the-world/use-of-ifrs-standards-by-jurisdiction/#analysis-introduction. [63]

IOSCO (2021), *Media Release 10/2021*, https://www.iosco.org/news/pdf/IOSCONEWS599.pdf. [82]

IOSCO (2021), *Report on Sustainability-related Issuer Disclosures*, https://www.iosco.org/library/pubdocs/pdf/IOSCOPD678.pdf. [58]

IPCC (2021), *Summary for Policymakers*, Cambridge University Press., https://www.ipcc.ch/report/ar6/wg1/#SPM (accessed on  August 2021). [1]

IPCC, I. (2018), *Global warming of 1.5°C: Summary for Policymakers*, https://www.ipcc.ch/. [2]

Johnson, P. (2018), *Global Philanthropy Report: perspectives on the global foundation sector*, https://cpl.hks.harvard.edu/files/cpl/files/global_philanthropy_report_final_april_2018.pdf. [67]

Kalemli-Ozcan, S., L. Laeven and D. Moreno (2019), *Debt Overhang, Rollover Risk, and Corporate Investment: Evidence from the European Crisis*. [47]

Littenberg et al., E. (2020), *Delaware Public Benefit Corporations—Recent Developments*, https://corpgov.law.harvard.edu/2020/08/31/delaware-public-benefit-corporations-recent-developments/ (accessed on 25 August 2021). [38]

L'Observatoire des Sociétés à Mission (2021), *Portrait des sociétés à mission*, https://uploads-ssl.webflow.com/5f0482651f0a7d3558f6a617/614993bd744273e674fab8c7_OSAM_Troisieme_Barometre.pdf (accessed on  September 2021). [39]

LSE, G. (ed.) (2020), , https://climate-laws.org/ (accessed on 20 August 2021). [41]

Lu, W. and M. Taylor (2016), *Which Factors Moderate the Relationship between Sustainability Performance and Financial Performance?*. [99]

McClane, J. (2019), "Boilerplate and the Impact of Disclosure in Securities Dealmaking", *Vanderbilt Law Review*, Vol. 72, pp. 191-295, https://scholarship.law.vanderbilt.edu/vlr/vol72/iss1/7. [55]

McKinsey & Co. (2019), *More than values: The value-based sustainability reporting that investors want*, https://www.mckinsey.com/~/media/McKinsey/Business%20Functions/Sustainability/Our%20Insights/More%20than%20values%20The%20value%20based%20sustainability%20reporting%20that%20investors%20want/More%20than%20values-VF.pdf. [61]

Morrow Sodali (2021), *Institutional Investor Survey 2021*, https://morrowsodali.com/insights/institutional-investor-survey-2021. [9]

NGFS (2019), *A call for action: Climate change as a source of financial risk*, https://www.ngfs.net/sites/default/files/medias/documents/synthese_ngfs-2019_-_17042019_0.pdf. [11]

NY Times (2021), *Exxon's Board Defeat Signals the Rise of Social-Good Activists*, https://www.nytimes.com/2021/06/09/business/exxon-mobil-engine-no1-activist.html (accessed on 23 August 2021). [37]

OECD (2021), *OECD Sovereign Borrowing Outlook 2021*, OECD Publishing, Paris, https://doi.org/10.1787/23060476. [75]

OECD (2021), *The Future of Corporate Governance in Capital Markets Following the COVID-19 Crisis*, OECD Publishing, Paris, https://doi.org/10.1787/efb2013c-en. [46]

OECD (2020), *OECD Business and Finance Outlook 2020: Sustainable and Resilient Finance*, OECD Publishing, Paris, https://doi.org/10.1787/eb61fd29-en. [66]

OECD (2018), *Flexibility and Proportionality in Corporate Governance*, OECD Publishing, Paris, https://doi.org/10.1787/9789264307490-en. [62]

OECD (2018), *OECD Due Diligence Guidance for Responsible Business Conduct*, https://mneguidelines.oecd.org/due-diligence-guidance-for-responsible-business-conduct.htm. [56]

OECD (2017), *Investing in Climate, Investing in Growth*, OECD Publishing, Paris, https://doi.org/10.1787/9789264273528-en. [70]

OECD (2011), *OECD Guidelines for Multinational Enterprises*, http://mneguidelines.oecd.org/guidelines/. [42]

OECD (2010), *Corporate Governance and the Financial Crisis*, https://www.oecd.org/daf/ca/44679170.pdf. [54]

OJK (2021), *Regulation of Financial Services Authority NO. 51/POJK.03/2017 on Application of Sustainable Finance to Financial Services Institution, Issuer and Publicly Listed Companies*, https://www.ojk.go.id/id/kanal/perbankan/regulasi/peraturan-ojk/Documents/Pages/POJK-Penerapan-Keuangan-Berkelanjutan-bagi-Lembaga-Jasa- [95]

Keuangan,-Emiten,-dan-Perusahaan-Publik/SAL%20POJK%2051%20-%20keuangan%20berkelanjutan.pdf.

Pew Research Center (2021), *In Response to Climate Change, Citizens in Advanced Economies Are Willing To Alter How They Live and Work*, https://www.pewresearch.org/global/2021/09/14/in-response-to-climate-change-citizens-in-advanced-economies-are-willing-to-alter-how-they-live-and-work/. [33]

Ratsimiveh, K. et al. (2020), *ESG scores and beyond: Factor control: Isolating specific biases in ESG ratings*, FTSE Russell, https://content.ftserussell.com/sites/default/files/esg_scores_and_beyond_part_1_final_v02.pdf. [23]

Roe, M. (2018), "Stock Market Short-Termism's Impact", *U. Pa. L. Rev.*, https://scholarship.law.upenn.edu/penn_law_review/vol167/iss1/3. [44]

S&P Global (2019), *Exploring the G in ESG: Governance in Greater Detail – Part I*, https://www.spglobal.com/en/research-insights/articles/exploring-the-g-in-esg-governance-in-greater-detail-part-i (accessed on September 2021). [21]

SASB (2017), *SASB Conceptual Framework*, https://www.sasb.org/wp-content/uploads/2020/02/SASB_Conceptual-Framework_WATERMARK.pdf. [107]

SASB (2017), *SASB Rules of Procedure*, https://www.sasb.org/standards/rules-of-procedure/. [106]

SASB Standards Board, GSSB, <IR> Framework Board, CDSB and CDP (2020), *Reporting on enterprise value*, https://29kjwb3armds2g3gi4lq2sx1-wpengine.netdna-ssl.com/wp-content/uploads/Reporting-on-enterprise-value_climate-prototype_Dec20.pdf. [18]

Science Based Targets Initiative (2021), *How-To Guide for Setting Near-Term Targets*, https://sciencebasedtargets.org/resources/files/SBTi-How-To-Guide.pdf. [27]

SEBI (2021), *Circular - Business responsibility and sustainability reporting by listed entities*, https://www.sebi.gov.in/legal/circulars/may-2021/business-responsibility-and-sustainability-reporting-by-listed-entities_50096.html. [93]

SEC (2022), *Press Release: SEC Proposes Rules to Enhance and Standardize Climate-Related Disclosures for Investors*, https://www.sec.gov/news/press-release/2022-46. [86]

SEC (2010), *Comission Guidance Regarding Disclosure Related to Climate Change*, https://www.sec.gov/rules/interp/2010/33-9106.pdf. [83]

Setzer J and Higham C (2021), *Global trends in climate change litigation: 2021 snapshot*, https://www.lse.ac.uk/granthaminstitute/wp-content/uploads/2021/07/Global-trends-in-climate-change-litigation_2021-snapshot.pdf. [40]

Skog, R. (2015), *The Importance of Profi t in Company Law – a Comment from a Swedish Perspective*, De Gruyter, pp. 563-571. [31]

Strine Jr., L. (2017), "Who bleeds when the wolves bite? A flesh-and-blood perspectuve on hedge fund activism and our strange corporate governance system", *Yale Law Journal*, Vol. 126, p. 1870, https://papers.ssrn.com/sol3/papers.cfm?abstract_id=2921901. [45]

Stubbington, T. (2021), *Squeeze on 'greenium' as ESG bond investors demand more value*, [73] https://www.ft.com/content/ecbed322-1709-4ed6-9f7f-d974f6e181da.

Suncor Energy (2021), *Report on Sustainability*, https://sustainability.suncor.com/en. [59]

Taylor, B. (2020), "Send bond covenants into battle against climate change", *Financial Times*, https://www.ft.com/content/0472f192-00e3-4119-a8a7-c5b1a379fbce (accessed on September 2021). [102]

TCFD (2021), *2021 Status Report*, https://www.fsb.org/2021/10/2021-status-report-task-force-on-climate-related-financial-disclosures/. [15]

TCFD (2020), *2020 Status Report*, https://www.fsb.org/2020/10/2020-status-report-task-force-on-climate-related-financial-disclosures/. [103]

TCFD (2020), *Guidance on Scenario Analysis for Non-Financial Companies*, https://assets.bbhub.io/company/sites/60/2020/09/2020-TCFD_Guidance-Scenario-Analysis-Guidance.pdf. [12]

TCFD (2017), *Recommendations of the Task Force on Cl imate related Financial Disclosures*, https://www.fsb-tcfd.org/recommendations/. [10]

The Investment Association (2021), *Letter to the Remuneration Committee Chair*, https://www.theia.org/sites/default/files/2021-11/Rem%20Com%20Chair%20letter%20-%20Final.pdf. [26]

TSVCM (2021), *Taskforce on Scaling Voluntary Carbon Markets - Final Report*, https://www.iif.com/tsvcm. [77]

UK Department for Business, Energy and Industrial Strategy (2021), *Press release: UK to enshrine mandatory climate disclosures for largest companies in law*, https://www.gov.uk/government/news/uk-to-enshrine-mandatory-climate-disclosures-for-largest-companies-in-law (accessed on 23 December 2021). [88]

UK FCA (2022), *MIFIDPRU Remuneration Code*, https://www.handbook.fca.org.uk/handbook/SYSC/19G/?view=chapter. [87]

UN (2021), *Nationally determined contributions under the Paris Agreement*, https://unfccc.int/process-and-meetings/the-paris-agreement/nationally-determined-contributions-ndcs/nationally-determined-contributions-ndcs/ndc-synthesis-report#eq-5. [5]

UN (2021), *Net Zero Coalition*, https://www.un.org/en/climatechange/net-zero-coalition (accessed on 20 December 2021). [4]

UN (2021), *The Glasgow Climate Pact – Key Outcomes from COP26*, https://ukcop26.org/wp-content/uploads/2021/11/COP26-Presidency-Outcomes-The-Climate-Pact.pdf. [6]

UN (2015), *United Nations Framework Convention on Climate Change*, http://unfccc.int/files/essential_background/convention/application/pdf/english_paris_agreement.pdf. [3]

US SEC (2021), *CF Sample Letter to Companies Regarding Climate Change Disclosures*, https://www.sec.gov/corpfin/announcement/announcement-sample-letter-climate-change-disclosures (accessed on 23 December 2021). [85]

US SEC (2021), *Press Release: SEC Announces Annual Regulatory Agenda*, [84] https://www.sec.gov/news/press-release/2021-99 (accessed on 23 December 2021).

WEF (2020), *Embracing the New Age of Materiality: Harnessing the Pace of Change in ESG*, https://www.weforum.org/whitepapers/embracing-the-new-age-of-materiality-harnessing-the-pace-of-change-in-esg. [57]

Wheelan, T. et al. (2021), *ESG and Financial Performance:*, https://www.stern.nyu.edu/sites/default/files/assets/documents/NYU-RAM_ESG-Paper_2021%20Rev_0.pdf. [20]

# Annex A. Selected indicators for sustainability issues

Table A.1. Selected indicators for sustainability issues where risks are likely to be financially material in 2021

| Dimension | Sustainability Issues | Share of market capitalisation of industries where the risk is material (in total global market cap.) | Number of industries where the risk is material (out of a total of 77) |
|---|---|---|---|
| Environment | Energy Management | 47% | 33 |
| | GHG Emissions | 27% | 25 |
| | Water & Wastewater Management | 26% | 25 |
| | Waste & Hazardous Materials Management | 21% | 19 |
| | Air Quality | 15% | 17 |
| | Ecological Impacts | 9% | 14 |
| Social Capital | Data Security | 38% | 15 |
| | Product Quality & Safety | 26% | 26 |
| | Selling Practices & Product Labelling | 19% | 15 |
| | Access & Affordability | 19% | 8 |
| | Customer Privacy | 19% | 6 |
| | Human Rights & Community Relations | 14% | 6 |
| | Customer Welfare | 12% | 14 |
| Human Capital | Employee Engagement, Diversity & Inclusion | 38% | 12 |
| | Employee Health & Safety | 25% | 27 |
| | Labour Practices | 15% | 12 |
| Business Model & Innovation | Product Design & Lifecycle Management | 53% | 37 |
| | Materials Sourcing & Efficiency | 27% | 19 |
| | Supply Chain Management | 24% | 19 |
| | Business Model Resilience | 7% | 7 |
| | Physical Impacts of Climate Change | 6% | 8 |
| Leadership & Governance | Business Ethics | 27% | 18 |
| | Systemic Risk Management | 17% | 8 |
| | Critical Incident Risk Management | 10% | 14 |
| | Competitive Behaviour | 8% | 11 |
| | Management of the Legal & Regulatory Environment | 7% | 5 |

Source: OECD Capital Market Series Dataset, Factset, Thomson Reuters Eikon, Bloomberg, SASB mapping, and OECD calculations

# Notes

[1] It is acknowledged that ESG and sustainable investing encompass a wider range of issues than climate change and its associated risks. However, this report starts with these broader categories to provide an indication of the trends and magnitude of investor focus on ESG-related criteria, including climate change. With due consideration of the challenges involved in separating out data on climate-related investing alone, complementary sources of data that are more specific to climate change are also considered in the report.

[2] Funds retrieved from the Reuters Funds Screen were classified as Climate Funds or ESG Funds in cases where their names contain, respectively, climate or ESG relevant acronyms and words such as ESG, sustainable, responsible, ethical, green and climate (and their translation in other languages).

[3] According to another estimate, the impact investing market size worldwide (including emerging markets) was equal to USD 715 billion at the end of 2019 (GIIN, 2020[98]).

[4] With respect to environmental factors related to climate change, this value of assets under management might even be an underestimation, because some investors who do not have a clear sustainable investing mandate might nonetheless be concerned with their exposure to climate risks (and willing to engage with corporates to reduce their risks). For instance, 615 investors (including from emerging markets) with USD 60 trillion in assets under management have so far joined the Climate Action 100+, which is an initiative to ensure the world's largest corporate GHG emitters (currently, 167 focus companies representing more than 80% of global industrial emissions) cut emissions to help achieve the goals of the Paris Agreement (Climate Action 100+, 2021[105]).

[5] Companies sometimes make reference to the UN Sustainable Development Goals (the 2030 development agenda adopted by all UN members in 2015) and to the UN Global Compact (an engagement initiative with companies on human rights, labour, environment and anti-corruption) in their sustainability and mainstream filings. While relevant, they would not normally be considered as ESG accounting and reporting frameworks or standards per se.

[6] The eight industries are: banking; insurance; energy; materials and buildings; transportation; agriculture, food, and forest products; technology and media; and consumer goods. Companies were selected based on 2019 company size thresholds: banks and insurance companies with more than, respectively, USD 10 billion and USD 1 billion in assets; all other companies with more than USD 1 billion in revenues. Companies were removed from the sample if they did not have annual reports in English for all the three years under analysis.

[7] The difference between regions may be explained by different factors, but one to consider is the distribution by industries in each country. For instance, companies in the technology and media industry globally tend to report less often in line with TCFD recommendations (probably because the industry is

seen as relatively less exposed to climate-related risks), and the sample of North American companies was skewed toward the technology and media industry (TCFD, 2021, p. 36[15]).

[8] IAASB defines "assurance engagement" as "an engagement in which a practitioner expresses a conclusion designed to enhance the degree of confidence of the intended users other than the responsible party about the outcome of the evaluation or measurement of a subject matter against criteria" (2000, pp. 6, 13[104]). It includes both the audit of financial statements and engagements on a wide range of subject matters such as climate-related disclosure.

[9] The 100 largest companies by market capitalisation in The People's Republic of China, Germany, India, Japan, the United Kingdom and the United States, and the 50 largest in Argentina, Brazil, Canada, Mexico, France, Italy, Russia, Saudi Arabia, South Africa, Spain, Turkey, Australia, Hong Kong (China), Indonesia, Singapore and Korea.

[10] © 2021 Value Reporting Foundation. All Rights Reserved. OECD licenses the SASB SICS Taxonomy.

[11] SASB mapping serves as the organising structure for the SASB Standards. Each one of the 77 industries in the mapping has its own unique Standard, and the accounting metrics in each Standard are directly linked to the sustainability themes that were considered to be financially material to an industry in the mapping (SASB, 2017, pp. 16-17[107]). The changes in the SASB mapping and the SASB Standards are, therefore, intertwined in a structured standard-setting process. This process is based on evidence of both financial impact and investor interest, using both research by Value Reporting Foundation staff and consultation with companies and investors (SASB, 2017, pp. 13-16[106]). Any change in SASB Standards and its accompanying mapping goes through extensive due process, including being approved by a majority vote of the SASB Standards Board, which is composed of five to nine members with diverse backgrounds (e.g. experience and expertise in investing, corporate reporting, standard-setting and sustainability issues) (SASB, 2017, pp. 9-10[106]).

[12] SASB mapping does not include a risk category for GHG Scope 3 emissions.

[13] Classification in the table is made from a universe of listed companies consisting of 38 834 companies with a total market capitalisation accounting for almost 99% of all publicly listed companies worldwide. The universe covers all non-financial and financial companies and excludes all types of funds and investment vehicles including Real Estate Investment Trusts (REITs). The primary listing venue is taken into account when identifying the market where the company is listed. Secondary listings are not taken into account. The list of listed companies for each market contains only firms that trade ordinary shares and depositary receipts as their main security. Companies trading over-the-counter and on non-regulated segments are excluded.

[14] In the Annex of this document, a more comprehensive version of Table 1.5, including all sustainability issues from the SASB mapping, is presented.

[15] In addition to the paper detailed in this paragraph, a meta-analysis of 198 studies suggests that good sustainability practices likely increase a firm's financial performance, especially in the long run (Lu and Taylor, 2016[99]). A study of 25 meta-analyses found a highly significant, positive, robust and bilateral relation between sustainability and financial performances (Busch and Friede, 2018[100]).

[16] A review of 59 papers focused on the relationship between climate-related corporate results and corporate financial performance found a similar relationship as identified for ESG results more broadly: 57% arrived at a positive relationship, 9% mixed conclusions, 29% a neutral impact and 6% a negative impact (Wheelan et al., 2021, p. 2[20]).

[17] The total market capitalisation of these 7 801 listed companies as of end 2021 account for almost 82% of all publicly listed companies worldwide.

[18] The total market capitalisation of these companies account for almost 83% of all publicly listed companies.

[19] The index of 100 large UK-listed companies.

[20] The business judgement rule acts as a presumption that the board of directors fulfilled its duty of care unless plaintiffs can prove gross negligence or bad faith. Similarly, if a director had a conflict of interest, the court will not typically uphold the presumption.

[21] See more in https://www.nbim.no/en/the-fund/responsible-investment/ownership/.

[22] For a definition of Scopes 1, 2 and 3 emissions according to the GHG Protocol, please see notes to Table 1.3.

[23] Thomson Reuters Eikon, OECD calculations.

[24] These seven listed PBCs are Zevia PBC, Mpower Financing Public Benefit Corp., Veeva Systems, Lemonade Inc, Vital Farms, Laureate Education Inc., and Appharvest Inc.

[25] The three listed *sociétés à mission* are Danone, Voltalia, and Realites. They had, respectively, market capitalisations of USD 45 billion, USD 2.3 billion and USD 106 million as of September 2021.

[26] 40 countries are included in the database (among others, Argentina, Australia, Brazil, Canada, most European countries, India, Indonesia, Japan, Mexico, Pakistan, South Africa and the US) and 13 regional or international jurisdictions. However, due to limitations in data collection (for instance, cases filed in US state courts are not covered), numbers may not include every climate case filed in all aforementioned jurisdictions.

[27] "Short-termism" could be defined as an investment-making process that favours projects with higher short-term cash inflows to the detriment of projects with longer-term payoffs, without properly considering the net present value of all possible investment projects.

[28] The TRWG is composed of representatives from the CDSB, the IASB, the Financial Stability Board's TCFD, the VRF and the World Economic Forum, and it is supported by IOSCO.

[29] The IAASB defines a "reasonable assurance engagement" as one in which "the practitioner reduces engagement risk to an acceptable low level in the circumstances of the engagement", while a "limited assurance engagement" is defined as one "limited compared with that necessary in a reasonable assurance engagement but [...] likely to enhance the intended users' confidence about the subject matter information to a degree that is clearly more than inconsequential" (IAASB, 2013, p. 7[101]).

[30] Some company laws merely mention that directors should act in the best interest of the company, but, evidently, companies are only fictional persons, and, therefore, regulators, courts and other practitioners will have to – in concrete cases –definewho the company effectively serves.

[31] As previously mentioned, if courts adopt the business judgement rule (or similar doctrines in non-US jurisdictions), they would review directors' decisions only in the relatively rare circumstances where plaintiffs can prove negligence or bad faith.

[32] Another layer in this discussion would be whether institutional investors (e.g. pension and mutual funds) would be able to consider non-financial goals of their final beneficiaries. In many developed jurisdictions, institutional investors are permitted (or may even be required in some cases) to integrate ESG issues into their investment decisions and ownership practices with the goal of maximising financial return (Freshfields, 2021[108]). However, pursuing an investment for non-value-related sustainability reasons would not likely be possible in the absence of a clear mandate from final beneficiaries. For instance, the US Department of Labor holds the view that employee benefit plans' fiduciaries are not permitted to sacrifice investment return or take on additional investment risk as a means of using plan investments to promote collateral social policy goals (Interpretive Bulletin 2015-01).

[33] OECD Capital Market Series Dataset.

[34] See, for instance, Regulation EU 2020/852 on the establishment of a framework to facilitate sustainable investment.

[35] In 2019, Enel, an Italian utility company, issued a corporate bond of which the covenants linked the coupon rate to the goal of making 55%of the energy company's overall installed capacity renewable by the end of 2021. If that target is not met (as reported by an independent auditor), the interest on the bond will increase by 25 basis points (Taylor, 2020[102]).

[36] The 14 jurisdictions are Australia, the European Union, France, Germany, Hong Kong (China), Indonesia, India, Italy, Japan, the Netherlands, Singapore, Spain, Turkey and the United Kingdom.

[37] See FCA (2020) Proposals to enhance climate-related disclosures by listed issuers and clarification of existing disclosure obligations.

[38] See https://www.fca.org.uk/firms/remuneration.

[39] The remuneration code for MIFIDPRU investment firms.

[40] Directive 2014/95/EU.

[41] The requirements would cover nearly 50 000 companies, defined as companies that meet two of the following three criteria: 1) a balance sheet of more than EUR 20 million; 2) turnover of more than EUR 40 million; 3) more than 250 employees.

[42] European Parliament and Council of the European Union (2019), Regulation of the European Parliament and of the Council on sustainability-related disclosures in the financial services sector, https://data.consilium.europa.eu/doc/document/ST-7571-2019-ADD-1/en/pdf.

[43] PRI-FrenchEnergyTransitionLaw.pdf (unepfi.org).

[44] France, Duty of Vigilance Law, https://www.legifrance.gouv.fr/eli/loi/2017/3/27/2017-399/jo/texte.

[45] See Environmental, Social & Governance Law 2021 | Australia | ICLG.

[46] See www.responsible-investor.com.

[47] See India Imposes New ESG Reporting Requirements on Top 1000 Listed Companies | Eye on ESG.

www.ingramcontent.com/pod-product-compliance
Lightning Source LLC
Chambersburg PA
CBHW081202270326
41930CB00014B/3266

* 9 7 8 9 2 6 4 4 6 1 8 6 4 *